Praise for *We Shall All Be Changed*

No resource has provided m[...] my own battle with grief than *W*[...] re-counts the slow and at times ag[...] he brings clarity to both the pain [...] ......ung a loved one suffer, and throughout she guides her readers directly to the God of all comfort, who enters into our grief and prepares our hearts for heaven.

LYDIA BROWNBACK, author of several books, including the Flourish Bible Study series, and Bible teacher with a Master of Arts in Religion from Westminster Theological Seminary

I've known Whitney for as long as her mother battled cancer. And what she offers us in *We Shall All Be Changed* is the insight and wisdom gained through suffering well for a long time. With honesty, transparency, and a deep love of God, Whitney invites us to lift our eyes and see the comfort of the Lord in the midst of deep grief, the goodness of the Lord in the midst of great sorrow, and the presence of the Lord in the moments of profound pain. I have no doubt that the Lord will use Whitney's story to comfort and strengthen you in yours.

COURTNEY DOCTOR, Director of Women's Initiatives for The Gospel Coalition, Bible teacher, and author of *From Garden to Glory*, *In View of God's Mercies*, and others

In a broken world, still riddled with the effects of sin, we all walk through seasons of suffering and pain. In my own seasons of suffering, I wish I would've had Whitney Pipkin's *We Shall All Be Changed*. This is a resource that is theologically rich, biblically serious, and deeply human. I am praying this book gets a wide reading as it will help all of us on our journeys of suffering by pointing us to the God who is making all things new.

JT ENGLISH, lead pastor of Storyline Church, author of *Deep Discipleship*, coauthor with Jen Wilkin of *You Are a Theologian*, and cohost of the *Knowing Faith* podcast

By God's grace, *We Shall All Be Changed* came to me in a season of caring for my mother, suffering from Alzheimer's. This beautifully written book gave me language both for grief and hope. As each page turned, I was reminded to look to my brokenhearted Savior and find His help in this present trouble. If you're keeping vigil, if you feel yourself wrecked by sudden or slow loss, let this book lead you through—and beyond—the valley of the shadow of death.

JEN POLLOCK MICHEL, author of *In Good Time* and *A Habit Called Faith*

I won't forget this book. *We Shall All Be Changed* is a stunningly beautiful and powerful story of caring for someone who is dying. Whitney's honesty and theological depth will ease your fears of death, either your own or that of a loved one, realizing that the journey will deepen us and that endless glory awaits.

VANEETHA RISNER, author of *Desperate for Hope* and *Walking Through Fire*

In prose at turns poignant, profound, and achingly beautiful, *We Shall All Be Changed* offers the grieving and the weary a cool cup of water. Much ink has been spilled on death and grief, but seldom do such treatises combine the vulnerability, candor, and theological rigor of Pipkin's work. She expertly weaves personal experience with careful research and biblical insight to guide the hurting on a journey toward hope and healing—on a journey toward the solace that only a Savior acquainted with grief can bring. While intended for those facing death and loss, readers in *all* seasons of life will benefit from the wisdom and theological riches in these pages."

KATHRYN BUTLER, author of *Between Life and Death*, *Glimmers of Grace*, and The Dream Keeper Saga

Whitney Pipkin's profound twenty-year journey—walking with her mother through cancer, confronting death head-on, delving into the depths of our souls, and emerging with rich hope in Jesus—is masterfully captured in *We Shall All Be Changed*. Her meditation in the house of mourning produced a heart of wisdom, which she generously shares with us in this remarkable book. With unwavering candor, Pipkin weaves her story with biblical insight, creating a luminous roadmap for all who will, are, or have walked with loved ones to the grave.

ERIC M. SCHUMACHER, author of *Ours: Biblical Comfort for Men Grieving Miscarriage* and the novella *My Last Name*

In *We Shall All Be Changed*, Whitney takes on a topic we too often avoid but must eventually confront head-on, masterfully weaving together tender personal stories and rock-solid theological truths. I found myself moved to tears several times while reading, simultaneously flooded with memories of my own up-close experience with death *and* comforted again and again by the gospel of Jesus.

CAROLINE COBB, singer-songwriter and author of a forthcoming Advent devotional

As one of Whitney's pastors, I know this book isn't theoretical. It's the fruit of biblical truth that took root in her heart as she walked with Jesus and her mother through the valley of the shadow of death. Personally, my father died not long after Whitney's mother (on the one-year anniversary of her loss), and this book has been tremendous in my own processing of grief. I cannot wait for our covenant members to have her book in hand.

STUART MCCRAY, associate pastor at Grace Bible Church in Lorton, VA

As I'm preparing my thoughts to preach at the funeral of a friend's father, I'm reminded that *We Shall All Be Changed* is a gift to those who mourn and those who will mourn. I've known Whitney and her family, as their pastor, for more than a decade, and I've seen her walk through the fog of grief with arms outstretched to receive God's comfort, wisdom, and grace. In these pages she humbly, generously, and warmly recounts biblical truths that have been transforming for her, and will be for you, as we walk together into the house of mourning to see our glorious Savior reigning over death and leading us through the valley of death's shadow.

DOUG SACHTLEBEN, lead pastor at Grace Bible Church in Lorton, VA

I read this book after losing my father. In Whitney's beautiful prose and deep faith, I found ways to see deeper within myself and chart a course for the future. This book is a powerful guide and an indispensable companion for life's most universal experience: processing loss and finding a new way forward.

DANIEL STONE, bestselling author of *The Food Explorer* and *Sinkable*; former National Geographic journalist

We Shall All Be Changed

How Facing Death with Loved Ones Transforms Us

WHITNEY K. PIPKIN

MOODY PUBLISHERS
CHICAGO

Unless otherwise indicated, all Scripture quotations are from The ESV® Bible (The Holy Bible, English Standard Version®), copyright © 2001 by Crossway, a publishing ministry of Good News Publishers. Used by permission. All rights reserved.

Scripture quotations marked (NIV) are taken from the Holy Bible, New International Version®, NIV®. Copyright © 1973, 1978, 1984, 2011 by Biblica, Inc.™ Used by permission of Zondervan. All rights reserved worldwide. www.zondervan.com The "NIV" and "New International Version" are trademarks registered in the United States Patent and Trademark Office by Biblica, Inc.™

Scripture quotations marked (NLT) are taken from the Holy Bible, New Living Translation, copyright ©1996, 2004, 2015 by Tyndale House Foundation. Used by permission of Tyndale House Publishers, Carol Stream, Illinois 60188. All rights reserved.

Scripture quotations marked (NLV) are taken from the New Life Version, Copyright © 1969 and 2003. Used by permission of Barbour Publishing, Inc., Uhrichsville, Ohio 44683. All rights reserved.

Scripture quotations marked (BSB) are taken from the Berean Standard Bible. The Holy Bible, Berean Standard Bible, BSB is produced in cooperation with Bible Hub, Discovery Bible, OpenBible.com, and the Berean Bible Translation Committee. This text of God's Word has been dedicated to the public domain.

Scriptures marked (KJV) are taken from the King James Version.

All emphasis in Scripture has been added.

Content at the beginning of chapter 7 is based on a post on the author's blog: https://www.whitneyk pipkin.com/blog/when-the-universe-is-stilled.

Published in association with The Bindery Agency, www.TheBinderyAgency.com.

Edited by Amanda Cleary Eastep
Interior and cover design: Kaylee Dunn
Cover art adapted from the painting *Iris Bouquet* by Ruth Preston Finnell, the author's grandmother. Cover design of butterfly copyright © 2023 by dariaustiugova/Adobe Stock (360928293). All rights reserved.

Library of Congress Cataloging-in-Publication Data

Names: Pipkin, Whitney K., author.
Title: We shall all be changed : how facing death with loved ones
  transforms us / Whitney K. Pipkin.
Description: Chicago, IL : Moody Publishers, [2023] | Includes
  bibliographical references. | Summary: "Walking through death with a
  loved one can be incredibly isolating and unsettling. But we can
  experience God's very presence in life's dark and deep valleys.
  Beautifully honest and theologically rich, Whitney reveals the
  mysterious way that God ministers to and transforms us through death and
  suffering"-- Provided by publisher.
Identifiers: LCCN 2023028579 (print) | LCCN 2023028580 (ebook) | ISBN
  9780802431721 | ISBN 9780802473066 (ebook)
Subjects: LCSH: Death--Religious aspects--Christianity. | Trust in
  God--Christianity. | Suffering--Religious aspects--Christianity.
Classification: LCC BT825 .P57 2023 (print) | LCC BT825 (ebook) | DDC
  236/.1--dc23/eng/20230914
LC record available at https://lccn.loc.gov/2023028579
LC ebook record available at https://lccn.loc.gov/2023028580

Originally delivered by fleets of horse-drawn wagons, the affordable paperbacks from D. L. Moody's publishing house resourced the church and served everyday people. Now, after more than 125 years of publishing and ministry, Moody Publishers' mission remains the same—even if our delivery systems have changed a bit. For more information on other books (and resources) created from a biblical perspective, go to www .moodypublishers.com or write to:

Moody Publishers
820 N. LaSalle Boulevard
Chicago, IL 60610

1 3 5 7 9 10 8 6 4 2

Printed in the United States of America

In memory of Mom,
the woman who always knew
I could do hard things
but never wanted me to have to.
This one's for you.

Contents

Introduction

So far dying is a lot like birthing. Waiting and watching
and groaning for what's next—yet never quite ready.
It is a stream of breathy, needy prayers. How long, O
Lord? And please not yet. And come, Lord Jesus, come.

I thumb these words into the notes section of my iPhone around
3:30 a.m., the night of a Thanksgiving that has been grueling
and thankless. I am sitting in an indigo-blue velvet chair we call
Mom's "throne," watching the too-slow rise and fall of her chest.

She deliberated over buying this chair for weeks before declaring it the crown jewel of her recently renovated bathroom, complete with a sit-down vanity. Now, the cozy armchair is serving
another purpose. It is a seat we can pull close enough, drifting in
and out of our own sleep, to hold Mom's hand as it becomes clear
she won't be getting out of bed again. Mom is dying.

I sit still in the dim light of the bedside lamp, listening to
the otherworldly whir of an oxygen machine. I am wondering
when they will come, these last breaths we've been told to expect.
Despite my bone-deep exhaustion, the thought of missing them
keeps me rooted to this chair, studying her fading frame. The hospice nurses, who were only brought in yesterday, told us about the

signs, told us the end would come soon. But the whole process is still shrouded in mystery. Keeping vigil is all I can do.

Being here at Mom's earthly end, as unpredictable as it feels, has become vital to me. We drove our family of five the twenty hours from Virginia to Kansas for what we thought might be Mom's last Thanksgiving; maybe, we thought, she'd make it to the new year. I know now what we are here for: to bear witness to all of her sixty-three years—to the import and gravity of them—by holding on to her as they end.

At her bedside, I am seeing firsthand how demanding dying can be. My body already feels wrung out by the work of caregiving, which I've shared with my sister and stepdad, her husband of nearly twenty-five years. Each day feels like carrying another person through a marathon. We know the finish line exists, but we don't know when it will arrive. With every painful step, my spirit longs all the more for Mom's suffering to end, for her new life to begin—and to walk with her across these unknown waters.

Momma is lying in bed now, propped nearly upright . . . I am more aware than ever of my own breath, of every chime of the grandfather clock.

My mom's final breaths came the Saturday after Thanksgiving 2020. After two decades of dreading it, I was surprised by so much of the dying process. Rather than wondering if God had abandoned us, as I thought I might, I tasted and saw something of the Lord there that I can barely describe—yet instantly recognized.

There is beauty tucked inside the death of a believer, like the blood-red amaryllis bloom hidden for months within a dull, brown bulb. In a flash, the reality we've held on to for so long is revealed to be but a dim mirror. The temporal gives way to the eternal, and we bear witness before it evaporates again.

There is at the bedside of a believer—along with the searing pain—a form of the glory that made Moses' face glow radiant, a taste of a God who turns the worst we can imagine and renders good from it, a grace that astonishes us even here, and a God who whispers, "See, I am doing a new thing!" (Isa. 43:19 NIV).

"Behold! I tell you a mystery. We shall not all sleep, but we shall all be changed" (1 Cor. 15:51).

What I witnessed in my mom's death that day is a theme I now sense reverberating across the pages of Scripture, a note I hear hummed in beloved, old hymns: the darkest night gives way to dawn. The seed that dies breaks open and bears fruit. Where there was only bleak Friday and bewildering Saturday, resurrection bursts in.

But that light is only made brilliant by its contrast. We do not get Easter without the noonday darkness of Golgotha. The death part of our story matters as much as the life. And it gives us words for so much of what we experience in our daily lives in a body and a world that still groan, that still wait for resurrection to break through.

Until then, death is a drumbeat thumping across our experience of this present world—a deep rhythm that does not jump out on its own but is always there, steadying us, sobering us. As I learn to hum and walk along with its melodies and limits, I find that death is not just a subject to be saved for the very end. As a thread woven into the fabric of our lives on earth, death has a great deal to teach us about living them.

This book is an invitation to consider death, even if you don't have to right now. Odds are you will soon. Someone you love is aging in a way that startles you every time you see them. Someone you know is sick or dying; perhaps your own bedside vigil has begun. Someone you care about—maybe it's you—is deeply afraid of not having enough time, not having enough answers, not being enough in the end.

When death comes, grief is inevitable. But there is more we can render from it than a feeling of loss. There is deep value in developing a theological category for deadly diagnoses, aging, war, and the ache of losing someone. This theology of suffering helps us put skin on the idea that God might still be good when all is going wrong.

Our culture gives us plenty of opportunities to ignore these trappings of a dying world, to swindle us with a story of our own permanence and immortality. But buying into that won't serve us in the long run. When we don't allow God to teach us as well as comfort us in the face of death, we miss out on the fullness of a faith that neither cowers before nor fast-forwards past death.

Thinking about death in light of its inevitability is not masochism; it is wisdom. Just like it helps to develop a theology of suffering before we dive headlong into it, it serves us to foster a theology of death before we are desperate for one.

How can God be good in the midst of death? How can a God who claims victory over death still allow it? How on earth do I grieve with hope?

I have not answered all of these questions, but I have felt them with my entire being over the more than twenty years since my mom was first diagnosed with cancer. The Spirit groans some of them for me now as I continue to wade through the grief of losing her presence on earth.

But I have also felt God's goodness in this valley of the shadow of death—where the one who cannot break His promises says He will be with us. When the questions threaten to overwhelm me, I find my heart redirected to the feet of a Savior who faced death for me and faces all of its vestiges with me.

Rather than wanting to run from discussions of death—as I did for so long—I now want to press into them, to wring from one of the hardest trials life has to offer every drop of sanctification and glory. I see now that having a front seat to my mom's final days has forever changed the ones I have left to live.

DEATH TEACHES US HOW TO LIVE

When we fail to address death, theologian J. I. Packer says, "we part company with the Bible, with historic Christianity, and with a basic principle of right living, namely, that only when you know how to die can you know how to live."[1]

It is something of a modern dilemma that we have to develop this theology of death in the first place. It may even seem morose to contemplate death if you might otherwise get away with ignoring it for a while longer.

Previous generations, of course, did not have a choice as to whether they would consider death. It screamed into their worlds

1. J. I. Packer, *God's Plans for You* (Wheaton, IL: Crossway, 2001), 201.

every time a child was born without modern medicine bolstering his or her odds of survival. It had a seat at every dinner table, when the main course wasn't an item picked up at a grocery store, but one brought to the feast through the death of a backyard farm animal. Churchgoers for centuries walked by adjacent cemeteries on their way to the front door on Sundays. The sight would have prepared them to worship while they still had breath in their lungs and, as they left, to live the rest of their days with the end in sight.

Aging and dying, like births, didn't occur in faraway nursing homes and hospitals. It was all right there in the room, in the church, in the city. There was no avoiding death and all its unpleasant accessories.

Today, we are often able to choose the vantage point from which we witness a loved one's death, if the decision isn't made for us. For decades, more and more people have chosen to keep it at arm's length.

In the year 2000, nearly half of deaths occurred in hospitals,[2] with some of the more gruesome tasks of end-of-life caregiving shared by trained nurses and staff. But, even before the COVID-19 pandemic threatened to bring death to all our doorsteps, that trend was beginning to be reversed. In 2019, for the first time since tracking began in the 1970s, more people died at home than in hospitals.[3]

---

2. "QuickStats: Percentage of Deaths, by Place of Death - National Vital Statistics System, United States, 2000–2018," Centers for Disease Control and Prevention, May 15, 2020, https://www.cdc.gov/mmwr/volumes/69/wr/mm6919a4.htm.

3. Gene Emery, "Home Is Now the Most Common Place of Death in the US," *Reuters*, December 11, 2019, https://www.reuters.com/article/us-health-dying-choices/home-is-now-the-most-common-place-of-death-in-the-u-s-idUSKBN1YF2Q6.

Few people have the opportunity to be told when and how they might die. Those who do know are the product of modern medicine and dreaded-yet-helpful terminal diagnoses. A growing industry formed around end-of-life care now enables loved ones to end their days in their homes, if they wish.

Surveys have shown that nearly 80 percent of people would prefer to take their final breaths at home.[4] Of the 20 percent who don't, many cited concerns that they would be a burden to their family.

But perhaps we are beginning to notice that our cultural obsession with avoiding death doesn't serve us well. Maybe one of the lessons of a pandemic that left people dying alone in hospital rooms with their families on FaceTime is that we never, ever want to do that again. That walking with people through their hardest, final days is worth doing—or at least being able to do.

Even if you emerged from the coronavirus pandemic without seeing death up close, your eyes were surely opened to its ever-presence. Death is not just the endpoint of life; it is woven throughout. It is a thousand commas strewn across our days reminding us that we, that those we love, that the world we inhabit, are all in a process of dying.

Death is a hawk dangling limp from a chain link fence that stood between him and his prey. It is the grass you have watered and coddled all summer withering when you go out of town. It is

---

4. "Where Do Americans Die?," Stanford School of Medicine, Multi-Cultural Palliative Care, https://palliative.stanford.edu/home-hospice-home-care-of-the-dying-patient/where-do-americans-die.

leftovers languishing in the back of the fridge. It is a sudden gust of wind causing a tree branch to fall on the new car. It is technology wearing out and skin sagging beneath the weight of time. As Tish Harrison Warren writes in *Prayer in the Night*:

> I fill up my life with a thousand other things to avoid noticing the shadow of death. But I can't shake it. I bump up against it in big and small ways each day. Sleep, sickness, weariness, and nighttime itself are ordinary and unbidden ashes on our foreheads. They say to us: remember that you are going to die. And these daily tokens of mortality are then transformed, by God's mercy, into tools for good works.[5]

Somehow, this is good news. Because, as John Lennon quipped and Sandra McCracken has movingly sung, "If it's not okay, then it's not the end."[6] If death is still around, still seeming to reign, then we are still living between the already and the not-yet,[7] suspended here.

Seeing the end from the beginning—remembering the end in the middle—and considering death more fully helps us put the gut-wrenching present into context. This is not the end.

The fact that death is common to man is, in some ways, part of God's common grace. Had God not numbered their days

---

5. Tish Harrison Warren, *Prayer in the Night: For Those Who Work or Watch or Weep* (Downers Grove, IL: InterVarsity Press, 2021), 122.

6. The quote is most often attributed to John Lennon. Sandra McCracken sang of it in the song "Fool's Gold," track 1 on the album *Songs from the Valley* (Towhee Records, 2018).

7. As Got Questions Ministries explains, the phrase "already but not yet" refers to the way believers in this present age think of the kingdom and coming of God: "We are 'already' in the kingdom, but we do 'not yet' see it in its glory," https://www.gotquestions.org/already-not-yet.html.

by removing them from the garden's tree of life, Adam and Eve would have lived forever in a sin-soaked state. Those of us who have witnessed the whole-person impact of a prolonged sickness wouldn't wish for our loved ones to remain that way. There comes a point in their suffering, rather, where the end of it feels less like cruelty and more like kindness, like relief.

His grace is also in this: none of us is the first to face death and loss. We are not alone in experiencing its coming, in weeping over it. And the sweetest communion we will know in this shadowy vale is that of a suffering Savior. He not only tasted death for us, He weeps with us as we face it. When we fall into the pit of despair opened by these earthly losses, He does not call down to us from the safe ledge, as though we could pull ourselves out. He crawls into the pit with us. He holds us there.[8]

Scripture is not silent about death either. It rears its head in Genesis 3 and doesn't surrender until Revelation 21. Though death does not have the final word—though we know that one day God will put death to death—we live beneath its shadow for now.

DEATH IS A DOORWAY

For what it's worth, I am an unlikely person to be lecturing anyone about being comfortable with discussions of death and sickness. When we were younger, I was the one who had to leave the room when the needles came out while my sister, Alli, stayed to hold Mom's hand. I was the one who, for years, didn't want to

---

8. For more on this concept, consider the book by Dane Ortlund, *Gentle and Lowly: The Heart of Christ for Sinners and Sufferers* (Wheaton, IL: Crossway, 2020).

talk about it, didn't want to think about it, didn't want to do the fire drill of "What if?" until I really had to.

This was especially true during the years I was pregnant with each of our children, and grieving pregnancy losses in between. It was as if my body couldn't bear to carry life and death at the same time, so strong was my aversion to Mom's spiraling diagnosis during those years. I wonder now if I missed out, if life would have been a little richer had I walked with my eyes and heart a little more open, a little less scared.

This denial, if you want to call it that, is not something I easily shed. As the cancer my mom arm-wrestled for two decades took its toll, it became harder and harder for me to look at her. Over her last six or so years, as countless treatments wiped her hair away and bid it to never fully return, I have only a scant collection of pictures of her holding my children, all three of whom arrived during that time period. Many of them are subconsciously cropped to exclude the top of her bald or wispy-haired head. On some deep level, I knew that the lack of hair was linked to the story of her impending death—to treatment after treatment that, one by one, represented fewer options between her and its full arrival.

It wasn't until the end that I looked at her again, truly looked at her. There was no ignoring it now. Death was here. This was not a drill.

The thing I had feared the most—the great enemy, death— was still in many ways just that. I knew it was taking her from us. But as I faced it, however reluctantly, I was surprised to find another truth in its depths: death was also becoming her great deliverance. And she seemed all the more radiant as it drew near.

In some unexpected yet familiar way, the dreaded dead end became, as we blinked before it, the Red Sea Road[9] to all we had hoped would come true. It is in this odd way that the day of my mom's death surprised me. I had nearly forgotten, until it came, that it would also be a day of dawning glory.[10]

This is the way of the Christian life. This is the way, as *The Jesus Storybook Bible* says, everything sad comes untrue.[11] Somehow the blackest day in all of human history—the day of Christ's death—came to be called *Good* Friday.

Somehow, the day of my mom's death can be terrible and good at the same time too. Like the making of a new thing. Like the making of all things new. The very valley I feared most became the mountaintop from which I peered into the glory of God.

9. Ellie Holcomb, "Red Sea Road," on the *Red Sea Road* album (Full Heart Music, 2017).

10. This glory believers enter is not their own but God's. And they will share in it in a far fuller sense when Christ returns and they receive glorified, resurrection bodies.

11. Sally Lloyd-Jones, *The Jesus Storybook Bible: Every Story Whispers His Name* (Nashville, TN: Zonderkidz, 2007), 347. This phrase is originally attributed to a question Samwise Gamgee asks Gandalf in *The Lord of the Rings* (chapter 4 of Book Six): "Is everything sad going to come untrue?"

ONE

On Learning in the Dry Land of Loss

----

*It felt like the world had divided
into two different types of people,
those who had felt pain and
those who had yet to.*[1]

—MICHELLE ZAUNER, *CRYING IN H MART*

A journal entry six months after Mom died . . .

Friday, June 25, 2021

These tides of grief are so unwelcome. I wish I could find an island to wash up on for a while, to bask in the goodness of a warm sun just far enough from these waves. I have tasted

----

1. Michelle Zauner, *Crying in H Mart* (New York: Alfred A. Knopf, 2021), 160.

it, sweet breaks from the pain, remembrances of joy. But the tide always comes for me again. It is always inconvenient.

This morning, it was swim lessons. Mom, you were the first one to plunge Cora's little baby face beneath the water now six years ago. I was terrified, but you insisted it would be fine. You taught swimming lessons as a teen; you wanted to teach her. And now she's finally getting it. She's plunging her whole head beneath the water to dive for plastic treasures, coming up for air and approval, wearing a beaming, toothless smile.

Momma, how you would celebrate her! How I ache for that over-the-top praise of yours, for Cora and Charlie and Ruby to hear it, to grow up with it seeping into their bones.

"Your grandma always knew you could do it," I say now, a sorry replacement for you. "She cheered for you louder and harder than anyone, do you know that? Do you remember that?" Lord, help them remember that.

I should write an article today. I should care for the baby today. I should put on makeup and stop crying, or stop crying and then put on makeup. I should do a thousand things, but all I want to do is crawl back into bed and ache. Maybe I'd fall asleep and see you in my dreams again, so real I hate to wake up. I hate remembering you're not here, Mom. I hate how that reality has gotten more real, more believable, over the past six months. I see your picture by my lamp when I wake up—the one of you holding newborn Cora, when you still had hair—and I remember why it's there, that you're not.

Yesterday, I thought I was okay. I remembered how hard it was, how much you were hurting, how tough our relationship was at times. I'm glad that part is over. But I still wish you were here for me—how selfish—and for Alli and for our kids. I wish you were a phone call or a FaceTime away. I wish I could believe that you're looking down and cheering from heaven. I think you're probably doing something better, consumed with the glory of doing what your soul was created to do. If you're cheering us at all, it's toward the true finish line, eyes fixed on the Author and Perfecter of our faith.

I know I can make it there without you here. But, boy, I wish I didn't have to.

The death of a parent is like losing the backdrop to your life halfway through the play. These people were the tangible reference points to where you came from and who you've become. They're your biggest earthly influences, for better or worse. To continue living motherless or fatherless in a world that's full of them feels, for a while, like walking around with your skin peeled off.

Yet, like sin itself, losing parents is common to man. If life goes as we have come to expect it in this broken world, in the order of time, each of us will bury our parents. We will have been prepared for this, or so we thought, by saying goodbye to pets when we were kids and to grandparents as we grew older. As the Mandalorian might say, "This is the way."[2]

---

2. In the television series, the heavy metal-clad Mandalorian and others in his order of service regularly say to one another, particularly about difficult things they must do: "This is the way." Jon Favreau, producer, *The Mandalorian* (2019-2023), Disney Plus.

But none of these losses is made easier by being commonplace. None of us is ever *ready* to witness the slow demise of a loved one or a sudden shocking departure. No—losing my mother's presence on this earth has blown a chasm in me that will never be closed. I was not at all done being mothered at age thirty-three. I see now that I never will be.

But this is to say that death is something we will all face. Sometimes it springs on us. Sometimes it gives us years of warning and worrying. Too often, it comes out of order, taking a child from a father, a mother from a young family, a friend from college days.

It is an utter tragedy when children die, full stop. It is shocking when young adults in the prime of their lives are taken, when spouses and children are left behind too. And it is an odd sort of shock to lose parents in their fifties or sixties.

They were *almost* so many things: *almost* retired, *almost* on that vacation, *almost* or, in my case, *only briefly* a grandparent. They had a good many years; they should have had many more.

In my inner circle of friends, I am among the first to go through this losing of a parent, though I know I will not be the last. I had been walking with the possibility of Mom's death for more than two decades by the time it came, but I still kept it at bay for as long as I could. When her death had come and gone, I emerged from the fog with a new perspective.

Weeks later, a friend was talking about her father who had treated her cruelly growing up, saying she didn't care if he ended up in a nursing home when the time came. My entire body bristled in response, and tears filled my eyes. There is nothing inherently wrong with the 'round-the-clock help many families require to care for loved ones, especially when their end stages stretch over many months or years. What made me ache was the indifference in her voice, which I know was a cover for so much pain.

"I know it will be hard," I told her, "but if I've learned anything from walking through those final days with my mom, it's that you don't want to miss it if you have the chance."

As believers in life after death, we have the opportunity to love even those who have not loved us well, to the very end. We can extend improbable grace because, "The Lord is not slow to fulfill his promise as some count slowness, but is patient toward you [and your loved ones], not wishing that any should perish, but that all should reach repentance" (2 Peter 3:9).

People change in unimaginable ways when death draws near, and we can be changed too through witnessing it. At least two of my grandparents were saved in their final days. People showed up to have the conversations and, by the work of God's Spirit amid deadly diagnoses, they were ready to receive it.

I am convinced that walking with our parents through their deaths is one of the kindnesses God has woven into our reality, stained as it is by sin. Just as we tend to become aware of our parents' fallibility before our own, we can rehearse our own mortality by being confronted first with theirs.

We don't need to wonder if we are "called" to walk with our parents through the sunsets of their lives; 1 Timothy 5:3–4 notes that such care is a primary outworking of godliness and "is pleasing in the sight of God." Rather, engaging in this process offers us a hands-on form of sanctification as we seek to serve at life's end the people who gave us life.[3] That's not to say it is easy. The dying process does not cause the difficulties in our parental relationships to disappear. Rather, it tends to expose them. But what is brought into the light can, by God's grace, also be dealt with, endured, and forgiven. Maybe it can even begin to be healed.

This is also true of all opportunities to draw near to the dying. Yes, it may come at a cost. It will take time and emotional energy to sit in the ash heap with your coworker as her new cancer diagnosis sinks in. It may stir up fears about the safety of your own child to put yourself in the shoes of the one who recently lost hers, to weep alongside the Spirit that groans with us in prayer.

But there is richness to be reaped here. Whether you offer the ministry of presence or of dropping off presents on the front-door stoop—just don't stay away. The darkest corners that seem the farthest from God are the places He delights to be and to work. These are also the places He desires to send His workers, for, to tweak a phrase from Matthew 9:37, the harvest is plentiful, but the co-sufferers are few.

This rehearsal of hardship is also necessary preparation for each of us, one that many of us miss out on in an effort to avoid thinking about death at all. But fully facing our loved ones' mortality helps us live within our own limitations as humans. I trust it will also help each of us, one day, face our own walk across the waters with more courage, remembering the faces of those who have gone before.

---

3. "'Truly, I say to you, as you did it to one of the least of these my brothers, you did it to me'" (Matt. 25:40).

NUMBERED DAYS

Facing our loved ones' deaths sobers us about the brevity of our own lives. In Psalm 90, Moses writes from the perspective of watching an entire generation expire in the desert:

> *The years of our life are seventy,*
> > *or even by reason of strength eighty;*
> *yet their span is but toil and trouble;*
> > *they are soon gone, and we fly away." (v. 10)*

In light of this, Moses—somewhat surprisingly—concludes that life is still very much worth living. He sees the boundary lines of birth and death, of sickness and frailty, as guardrails that keep us living for what truly matters in the years we have left. And he prays:

> *So teach us to number our days*
> > *that we may get a heart of wisdom." (v. 12)*

This gift of perspective is tucked inside the deaths of those around us, inside the rhythms of one generation giving way to the next. But far too many of us—myself included—have spent more time worrying about and fearing it than we have spent listening to its lessons.

Theologian J. Todd Billings writes in *The End of the Christian Life* of how his own terminal illness helped shape in him a more robust theology of death. He concludes that modern Christians have been shielded from the natural realities of death, in part by living in neighborhoods and worshiping in churches that are filled only with the young.

> When we block out the groans of others, we find ourselves unprepared when the time comes for our own groaning. We lack language for grief as we stand near the graves of our loved ones. We wonder why we didn't live differently, why we didn't understand that life is indeed short. . . . But the path of Christian discipleship involves honest and regular reminders of both our mortal limits and those of our loved ones and neighbors. The path of Christian discipleship involves moving *toward* the wound of mortality, not *away from it*.[4]

In this way, facing our parents' mortality before our own is a gracious part of God's design. This is especially true if they are believers. Like Christian in *The Pilgrim's Progress*, we can rehearse the reality of our parents' journey toward the Celestial City even as we traverse our own.[5] We can look forward to—truly long for—the day when we will be reunited with them in glory. And we can live the days until then in light of this dawning reality.

To the end that thinking about death—that hearing another person's story of walking near it—might embolden you all the more to engage, I offer my somewhat ordinary experience. I know only my own, and I trust that, as writer Jacqueline Woodson says, "The more specific we are, the more universal something can become."

4. J. Todd Billings, *The End of the Christian Life: How Embracing Our Mortality Frees Us to Truly Live* (Grand Rapids, MI: Brazos Press, 2020), 12.

5. We've been reading Helen L. Taylor's *Little Pilgrim's Progress: The Illustrated Edition* (Chicago: Moody Publishers, 2021) with our children.

"Life," she adds, "is in the details."[6]

So, a few details: On my mother's side, my great-grandmother lived to be one hundred years old. My grandma died two weeks before her eighty-eighth birthday, and my mother died at age sixty-three—two years after burying her own mom. Though modern medicine would tell me that each generation can live longer and more healthfully than the one before, my family tree tells another story.

While it's not prophecy, it is a story I want to heed. It's one that chastens me from triumphalism and guards me from being fatalistic too. I don't know the number of hairs on my head or days of my life, but God does. Knowing they are limited—though I know not their number—prompts me to pray, then, with the end of Psalm 90:

Make us glad for as many days as you have afflicted us,

   and for as many years as we have seen evil.

Let your work be shown to your servants,

   and your glorious power to their children.

Let the favor of the Lord our God be upon us,

   and establish the work of our hands upon us;

   yes, establish the work of our hands!" (vv. 15–17)

6. Sona Charaipotra, "National Book Award Winner Jacqueline Woodson Talks Brown Girl Dreaming," Parade.com, November 26, 2014, https://parade.com/356078/sonacharaipotra/national-book-award-winner-jacqueline-woodson-talks-brown-girl-dreaming.

A WORD ON THE REALITY OF DEATH

There's a reason we don't like talking about death. I am not going to pretend there is no fear as death draws near, whether it's our own or that of a loved one. We intuitively quake before it and rail against this last enemy.

Our minds cannot fully grasp what's beyond our present reality, let alone on the other side of death. When we lack coldhard facts in a world that demands them, fear flourishes. As for our hearts, death is a harsh reality for those it leaves behind. It threatens to break us asunder, to shake us to pieces, to make target practice out of our hearts, poking holes in the faith we thought was firm.[7]

But often, when we go to the Bible in the wake of death asking "Why?" its overarching storyline answers us with a different question: "Who?" Our grief and lament lead us, however painfully and slowly, to the Man of Sorrows Himself, a Savior so "acquainted with grief" that it defined Him (Isa. 53:3). He faced death when it took His friend Lazarus. He faced death as it took His own life. And He faces the fullness of it for us and with us.

Yes, Christ rose again, declaring (incredibly!) victory over death. But He still wept, *really wept*, at the tomb of Lazarus. He still cried, "My God, my God, why have you forsaken me?" during His own death on the cross (Matt. 27:46). Even after resurrection, "He who broke the bonds of death kept his wounds," writes Christian philosopher Nicholas Wolterstorff in *Lament for a Son*.[8]

---

7. "I was at ease, but he hath broken me asunder: he hath also taken me by my neck, and shaken me to pieces, and set me up for his mark." (Job 16:12 KJV)

8. Nicholas Wolterstorff, *Lament for a Son* (Grand Rapids, MI: Eerdmans, 1987), 92.

We too will be wounded when it comes to take those we love. We too will cry out. We will weep at the bedsides and gravesites of our beloved. We will tear up at the grocery store. We will cry at the playground and in the car. We will stumble on a memory and curl into a ball intermittently for months and years and lifetimes, even if we know that, one day, our Savior will wipe away every tear.[9] There is no tidy theology that will keep those tears from falling.

But our suffering in death need not be deepened by surprise. Paul used the phrase "do not be surprised" in his letters to the first-century churches while addressing the concepts of fiery trials and the return of Christ. John also told his readers not to be surprised if the world hates them.[10] They knew that being surprised by something that feels so theologically unsettling would only add to the weight of their sorrow.

Likewise, if we do not understand and have not tested the doctrines we claim—that God has pointed the arrows of His wrath not at us who deserve it but at His own Son to save us—then every trial can feel like a double trial, leaving us to wonder whether God is truly *for us* in the midst of it.[11] Death can leave us particularly vulnerable to this way of thinking, especially when it strikes sooner than our modern life expectancies predict. The grief that accompanies it hits each of us so uniquely that it can be disorienting and dangerously isolating.

---

9. Revelation 21:4.

10. See 1 Peter 4:12; 1 Thessalonians 5:4; and 1 John 3:13.

11. Rev. Kevin Twit, campus minister at Reformed University Fellowship at Belmont University, made this comment while introducing the song "O Love That Will Not Let Me Go" on *The Hymn Sing* album (Indelible Grace Music, 2010).

This is when it matters to believe in a Savior who not only conquered death, but also *experienced* it. "Surely he has borne our griefs and carried our sorrows" (Isa. 53:4a).

The promise in the valley of the shadow of death is not that we won't walk through it—there is no avoiding it—but that God is *with us* when we do (Ps. 23:4a). We are perhaps too familiar with Psalm 23 for this truth to bowl us over, but it should. In the valley of the shadow of death, God's with-ness both changes us and comforts us (v. 4b). And it lifts our eyes to the day when we will dwell in His presence forever (v. 6b).

If God's presence is promised in this valley of death, shouldn't that change our perspective of it as disciples of Christ? If God's story is all about His desire to dwell with us—and about us receiving a desire to dwell with Him in return—that makes the place where His presence is promised the climax of the story. It's not to be skipped over. It is to be soaked in.

TWO

Where the Boundary Lines Fall

Teach me in health to think of sickness,
in the brightest hours to be ready for darkness;
in life prepare me for death.
Thus may my soul rest in thee,
O immortal and transcendent one.[1]

—THE VALLEY OF VISION

In some ways, my sister and I should have been more prepared for our mother's death. It was a thought simmering on the back burner of our lives for most of our formative years, though we thought about it only as often as we had to.

I was in the seventh grade and my sister in the fifth when Mom first spoke the dreaded word to us one night after school. We were sitting on the robin's egg-blue sheets of her sleigh bed, not far from

---

1. Arthur Bennett, *The Valley of Vision: A Collection of Puritan Prayers & Devotions* (Edinburgh, UK: The Banner of Truth Trust, 1975), 71.

the piles of laundry we'd be roped into folding (or so we thought), waiting for what she had to tell us.

"Girls, I found a lump right here," she said, patting her chest, "and it's breast cancer."

Her voice faltered and her face creased with an emotion I couldn't identify at the time, but sensed was primal. We smelled it on her and inhaled it too: fear. Our papa, her dad, had recently died of lung cancer, so we knew the word, knew its power to take away the people we loved. But our *mom*?

We squeezed both of our growing frames onto her lap and clung there as tears streamed and pooled together on her pleated khakis. I remember feeling like she might evaporate from us at any moment, like the mere idea of her not being here forever was enough to make her disappear right away. Little girls can't help but take their mothers for granted, until, suddenly, they can't.

BOOKENDS

There are things I didn't understand as a little girl that I see now, looking back. Regardless of when they arrive, birth and death are the unavoidable bookends of human life in a fallen world. They hem us in. They humble us. Their dates are penned onto birth announcements and carved into headstones. Together, they are printed at the top of an obituary and, in between, an entire life unfolds.

As we muddle through the middle between our own bookends, these beginnings and endings arrive for countless others around us. Each new birth, each life-threatening diagnosis, and each sudden death interrupts us as a stark reminder that we had a starting point on this earth, and we have an expiration date.

As the preacher soberly says in Ecclesiastes, "All are from the dust, and to dust all return" (Eccl. 3:20).

Tim Keller noted in his book *On Death* that crossing these thresholds of birth and death—our first and last boundary lines—"tends to concentrate the mind."[2] A month after it was published, he was diagnosed with pancreatic cancer that would take his life in 2023.

"I spent a few harrowing minutes looking online at the dire survival statistics for pancreatic cancer, and caught a glimpse of *On Death* on a table nearby," he later wrote for *The Atlantic*. "I didn't dare open it to read what I'd written."[3]

In that book, Keller had written that death shakes us temporarily "free from absorption in the whirl of daily life [to] ask the big questions of the ages: Am I living for things that matter? Will I have what it takes to face this new stage of life? Do I have a real relationship with God?"[4]

We ask these questions not only when we encounter such milestones ourselves but also when others around us do. As a young girl, I watched my mom go through this with her own diagnosis. And I began, even then, my own long process of considering how God's goodness might dovetail with life's hardships.

As unwelcome as death is, especially when it takes those we love, it can contain this strange gift for those it leaves behind. It wakes us from our stupor. It whispers to each of us left reeling in its wake, "How, then, will I live?"

---

2. Part of Tim Keller's trio of short theological books, *On Birth*, *On Marriage*, and *On Death* (New York: Penguin Books, 2020), xvi.

3. Tim Keller, "Growing My Faith in the Face of Death," *The Atlantic*, March 7, 2021.

4. Keller, *On Death*, xii.

We think of these wake-up calls as particularly compelling for those who do not yet believe in a loving God, nor trust in His only Son for salvation. The deaths of dear loved ones—especially those witnessed from close proximity—are indeed opportunities to reconsider the claims of the Bible: that the God-man, Jesus Christ, lived the spotless life we could never manage, died the death we deserve, and rose from a grave that could not hold Him—proof that His sacrifice on our behalf was accepted by a holy God. He who trusts in this alone, Jesus said, "though he die, yet shall he live" (John 11:25).

But what about our loved ones who don't believe in this, yet die? What are those of us who do believe to make of these amplified feelings of loss? Paul said of his Jewish brothers who had rejected Christ that he had "great sorrow and unceasing anguish" over their rejection (Rom. 9:2). He even wished he could cut himself off from Christ for the sake of these brothers (v. 3).

Wayne Grudem writes in his chapter on death in *Systematic Theology* that the pain Christians feel over the loss of unbelievers is "very deep and real."[5]

"The sorrow we feel is not mingled with the joy of assurance that they have gone to be with the Lord forever," Grudem says. "Yet it also must be said that we often do not have absolute certainty that a person has persisted in refusal to trust in Christ all the way to the point of death."[6]

Facing death can bring the promises of the gospel into crystal

---

5. Wayne Grudem, *Systematic Theology: An Introduction to Biblical Doctrine* (Leicester, UK: Inter-Varsity Press, 1994), 815.
6. Ibid.

clarity, as it did for the penitent thief on the cross next to Christ. Often, we cannot know the outcome for another. But we can lean into the arms of a God who does not wish "that any should perish, but that all should reach repentance" (2 Peter 3:9), a God who is merciful, just, and impossibly patient.[7]

Even for those of us who believe the biblical creeds whole-heartedly, facing death forces us to examine them in a new way in the aftermath of a loss. We are left turning these truths over in our hands, looking to see if they still stick in the upside-down daze that follows the loss of a loved one or our own near-death experience.

In her book *Teach Me to Feel*, Courtney Reissig writes of growing up with death as a very distant reality. She didn't attend her first funeral until college, and even then, she was not close to the person who died. It wasn't until she lost two children to miscarriage and then nearly lost her own life and her son's to pregnancy complications that death began to change her outlook on life.

"In a matter of moments, my unborn son's life—and mine—were on a knife-edge. And I've never been the same," she writes in a chapter meditating on Psalm 116. "Now death no longer feels far off. Now it feels too close for comfort.... How can life be enjoyed when it can be snuffed out in an instant?"[8]

Whether we've been delivered from our own close encounter or have witnessed a loved one's death, these experiences alter

---

7. This does not mean we should indicate to others that our loved one believed when there was no such evidence. This would, Grudem says, "diminish the urgency of the need for those who are still alive to trust in Christ." Grudem, *Systematic Theology*, 816.

8. Courtney Reissig, *Teach Me to Feel: Worshiping Through the Psalms in Every Season of Life* (Epsom, UK: The Good Book Company, 2020), eBook, 141.

who we are. Our life now divides into the Before Times—when planning a trip or retirement didn't feel presumptuous—and the After Times—when hope for the future feels slippery and subject to change.

DEATH IS AN OPPORTUNITY[9]

As the world limped toward the end of a global pandemic in the early 2020s, I was far from the only one coming face to face with death.

Around the time my mom died in late fall of 2020, the United States was experiencing between 20 percent and 40 percent more deaths per week than average. In addition to deaths attributed to the coronavirus, the pandemic may have set the stage for "excess deaths" by limiting access to preventative medical care, mental health services, and cancer treatment.[10] For people like my mom who were surviving the end stages of cancer by hopscotching from one clinical trial to another, a months-long pause in cancer research may have shortened her life too. And she was not the only one.

To put these numbers another way: if you survived those years, it's likely you know someone who didn't—more likely than it had been in decades.

---

9. Some of this mirrors content I wrote for an article for the Ethics and Religious Liberties Commission: "What's at Stake When We Brush Past Death," April 11, 2022, https://erlc.com/resource-library/articles/whats-at-stake-when-we-brush-past-death/.

10. "Excess Deaths Associated with COVID-19," Centers for Disease Control and Prevention. See charts for weekly data: www.cdc.gov/nchs/nvss/vsrr/covid19/excess_deaths.htm.

An article in *Christianity Today* in early 2022 noted that such intrusions of death into our national consciousness have historically led to cultural and religious changes.[11] That seemed to be playing out during the pandemic as well.

In one survey, the percentage of people age forty and older who said that religion is "very important" in the funeral of a loved one went up in 2020 and 2021 for the first time in a decade. Until the pandemic, it had been declining nearly every year since 2012. But by 2021, 47 percent of people said they found religion "very important" in the funeral of a loved one, up from 35 percent in 2019.[12]

In a *New York Magazine* article written after the peak of pandemic losses in 2021, an atheist wrote about how it was making even her wonder if she should try church again. "Mostly I wanted a way to mourn," Sarah Jones wrote, "not just my own loss but the galloping mass death enveloping the world."[13]

Jones said she was raised to be "a strict conservative Christian" but that she abandoned this brand of evangelicalism that was, in her experience, not "good with mystery, or with death." Belief in an afterlife felt "too easy." And yet, she found herself searching for something *like* it when death took her grandfather and then a friend.[14]

---

11. Daniel Silliman, "As COVID-19 Death Tolls Rise, More Americans Want Religious Funerals," December 13, 2021, *Christianity Today*, https://www.christianitytoday.com/ct/2022/january-february/religious-funerals-rise-covid-memorial-study.html.

12. Ibid., referencing a survey conducted by the National Funeral Directors Association of the United States.

13. Sarah Jones, "An Atheist Reconsiders God in the Pandemic," *New York Magazine*, October 11, 2021.

14. Ibid.

"I didn't need answers, not immediately," she wrote, "but I wanted to know it was possible to find them if I worked hard enough to look.... I wanted to stretch out my arms to something, even if I couldn't tell what it was."[15]

There are few things that rattle us like death. I've found this to be true for both those who believe in eternal life after it and those who don't. We see at the end of another's life a preview of the end of our own, and it sobers us. It also provides an opportunity to consider anew what death has to teach us about life.

Ecclesiastes says it is *better* to go to a house of mourning than to go to a house of feasting—better to attend a funeral than a wedding. Why? "For death is the destiny of everyone; the living should take this to heart" (Eccl. 7:2 NIV).

We will encounter death, and it *will* cause us to think about God. How we think about death while we are alive has an outsized impact on how we live while we are alive. That is why our theology of death is worth considering, revisiting, and reshaping. (Hint: if you've thought about death at all, you already have one.)

A BRIEF THEOLOGY OF DEATH
(AND WHY YOU NEED ONE)

Each of us already has a way of thinking about God and ourselves as it relates to death. It is the framework we use to answer key questions: Why does death exist? Why must *I* die? Why does the Giver of life allow death at all?

---

15. Ibid.

The world offers us its own answers. And, if we labor under an un-examined faith, we are prone to adopt them too . . . almost by osmosis. We swim, after all, in a sea of quasi-religious quips about death. They tell us that death is *natural*—part of a Lion King-like circle of life. They lull us into believing that we are still relatively young, that death is always far off. Sometimes the lie comes from our own sinful desires to outlive our limitations. Often, it comes from a culture that worships being *forever young*. Other times, the lie of our longevity comes right from the lips of the serpent who first whispered it to Eve in the garden: "You will not surely die" (Gen. 3:4).

But the best the ruler of this world has to offer us in the face of death is distraction.[16] It is the modern prescription for so much that ails, and we overdose on it to our destruction. We drink down the myth of our immortality even as our bodies and the bodies of those we love begin to tell a different story.

Too often, Christians in the American West are no better than non-Christians at facing death. This is a modern tragedy. Not only do we not live in the full light and hope of what the Bible teaches about death, but many of us haven't even considered it fully.

As Paul tells the Corinthians, "If in Christ we have hope in this life only, we are of all people most to be pitied" (1 Cor. 15:19).

Indeed, the Bible offers us much more.

In his book *Remember Death: The Surprising Path to Living Hope*, pastor Matthew McCullough says he hadn't naturally given much thought to the subject. It wasn't until he was teaching through the Bible, verse by verse—as a young pastor to a young congregation,

---

16. "Satan, the ruler of this world, will be cast out" (John 12:31 NLT).

no less—that it became increasingly difficult to ignore Scripture's preoccupation with the subject.

"I knew of [the Bible's] focus on the problem of sin and the problem of eternal judgment," he writes. "What struck me was its focus on physical death—the fact that our lives in this world come to an end."[17]

The broad themes of death running through Scripture were not a coincidence. Instead, they were the antidote to what easily ailed his young congregants.

"I have come to see, as the pastor of young up-and-comers, how important death-awareness can be," he writes. Why? "When the reality of death is far from our minds, the promises of Jesus often seem detached from our lives."[18]

The Bible is not determined to distract us from the reality of death. Quite the opposite. Death is a ribbon running red across its pages, from the first bite of forbidden fruit in the garden[19] to the day when it will be declared "no more" (Rev. 21:4). And along the way, death is transformed—astoundingly—into deliverance by the One who faced its fullness for us.

DEATH AS A THEME

I promise not to turn this into a theological treatise, but I think it's helpful to zoom out here for a quick overview of the story of death

17. Matthew McCullough, *Remember Death: The Surprising Path to Living Hope* (Wheaton, IL: Crossway, 2018), 22–23. This book is an excellent resource if you want to learn more about developing a theology of death.

18. Ibid.

19. See Genesis 3:6.

in Scripture. The disorienting things we think, feel, and wonder about in this limited life. They have a place in the story of God and in Scripture's story of death. The categories I'm using here are based on the overarching storyline of Scripture—sometimes called the *metanarrative*—that breaks down into four major movements: creation, fall, redemption, and consummation.

Let's look a little more closely at what each of these means as it relates to the theme of death in Scripture.

Creation: Death was not natural

There is no mention of death in Genesis 1 because the world God created did not contain it. The creation, the creatures, and God's image bearers were not *made to die* but to live forever under the ever-expanding glory of God.[20]

There is some debate over whether Adam and Eve were truly immortal at creation or if they simply had the potential to become immortal because of their access to the tree of life in the garden. Saint Augustine used the following categories to describe the possibilities: Before the fall, it was *possible not* to die. After the fall it was *not possible not* to die. After consummation, it will be *not possible* to die.[21]

---

20. See Nancy Guthrie's book *Even Better Than Eden: Nine Ways the Bible's Story Changes* (Wheaton, IL: Crossway, 2018) for more: "We often talk about our desires for the future as the restoration of Eden or returning to Eden. But the reality is, the Eden we read about in Genesis 1 and 2 wasn't yet everything God intended for his creation. It was unsullied but incomplete. . . . Adam and Eve were not yet all that God intended for his people to be. They were sinless but not yet glorious, at least not as glorious as God intended them to become," 12.

21. Joshua Van Ee, "Was Adam Created Mortal or Immortal? Getting Beyond the Labels," May 31, 2018, Carl F. H. Henry Center for Theological Understanding, https:// henrycenter.tiu.edu/2018/05/was-adam-created-mortal-or-immortal-getting-beyond-the-labels.

If death is simply to be expected, merely an ecological recycling of carbon, why does everything in us rage at it and run from it? Because we know on some deep, cellular level that it is not what we were made for but is, as McCullough writes, "an intrusion, something fundamentally unnatural."[22] We were made not by some accidental phenomenon but by an intimate, eternal God— and in His image, no less.

Therefore, our sense of dignity in life and of deep loss in death can both be traced back to our origins in a death-free garden.

Eternity is set into human hearts, says the writer of Ecclesiastes (3:11). We were made, first and foremost, not for this sin-soaked world but for God, to live forever with Him and for His glory. Death feels like an affront to our original makeup because it is.

Fall: Death is the result of sin

Yet, from the very beginning, God was graciously *warning* humans about the deadly consequences of doing things their own way, doubting the goodness of the One who made them in His image. He told them it would lead to this phenomenon they had not yet experienced: death.

"You may surely eat of every tree of the garden, but of the tree of the knowledge of good and evil you shall not eat, for in the day that you eat of it *you shall surely die*" (Gen. 2:16–17).

God's abundant provision in the garden was sure. And so was the punishment for not believing in it. Though Adam and Eve did not immediately die after eating the fruit, death immediately

22. McCullough, *Remember Death*, 71.

became possible and prevalent. To cover over the sudden shame of Adam and Eve's nakedness, some of the animals Adam named had to die.

The deadly consequences of their sin didn't just result in the first animal deaths. Their sin escorted Adam, Eve, and all their descendants out of the garden, out of the presence of the tree of life, and into a world that is "passing away" (1 John 2:17). This same reality is now true for each of us: "Just as sin came into the world through one man, and death through sin . . . so death spread to all men because all sinned" (Rom. 5:12). And Psalm 51:5 says we are each now born "in iniquity."

Because of sin, Adam and Eve would not only one day experience physical death, but they instantly tasted spiritual death. In this world, sin always leads to some form of death: the death of a relationship, the death of a dream, or the death of a body that was once called "very good."[23]

"For the wages of sin is death," Romans 6:23 tells us, "but the free gift of God is eternal life in Christ Jesus our Lord."

See how God and sin are pitted against one another, just like life and death? If the holy God is the creator and sustainer of life, then sin causes death by separating us from that life-giving source.

Death is the outcome of sin and the endpoint of life in a fallen world, all of it tinged by these dual realities. But death does not have the final word.

---

23. "Then desire when it has conceived gives birth to sin, and sin when it is fully grown brings forth death" (James 1:15); "And God saw everything that he had made, and behold, it was very good" (Gen. 1:31).

Redemption: Death was defeated by Christ

Death is an insurmountable problem. It separates us from loved ones. It separates us from life. It separates us from God. So we cry out along with Paul, "Wretched man that I am! Who will deliver me from this body of death?" (Rom. 7:24).

And we hear afresh the answer, "Thanks be to God through Jesus Christ our Lord!" (Rom. 7:25).

God's answer to the problem of death was to take it on Himself. Christ Jesus, "though he was in the form of God . . . humbled himself by becoming obedient *to the point of death*, even death on a cross" (Phil. 2:5–8).

Scripture's story holds its breath and finds its crescendo here, in the death of Christ. He is the ram caught in the thicket and tied to the altar instead of us. He is the ark in which we take refuge when the flood of judgment comes. He is the anointed King who defeats the giant that left us cowering.[24]

"He was *delivered over to death* for our sins" (Rom. 4:25a NIV). But what happened next? Did Christ remain dead? No, He "was *raised to life* for our justification" (Rom. 4:25b NIV). Jesus Christ did not—indeed, *could not*—stay dead.[25] On the third day, He rose in victory over the grave, proving that His spotless sacrifice was sufficient.

We will consider in a later chapter what Christ's victory over

---

24. This concept of finding Christ at the center of Old Testament salvation stories was the focus of The Gospel Coalition Women's Conference in June 2022. Learn more about these themes through the resource, Courtney Doctor and Melissa B. Kruger, *Remember Your Joy: A Bible Study of Salvation Stories in the Old Testament* (Wheaton, IL: Crossway, 2022).

25. "God raised him up, loosing the pangs of death, because it was not possible for him to be held by it" (Acts 2:24).

death really means for us now. But know this: "If the Spirit of him who raised Jesus from the dead dwells in you, he who raised Christ Jesus from the dead will also give life to your mortal bodies through his Spirit who dwells in you" (Rom. 8:11).

For those who find life in the gospel of Christ's finished work on the cross, the death sentence is lifted. There is no condemnation left. The One who holds the keys of death said "It is finished" on the cross and now says, "I am the Living One; I was dead, and now look, I am alive for ever and ever!"[26]

Consummation: Death will one day be no more

And yet, death remains part of our daily reality on this earth.

"Until Christ returns, all of us will grow old and die," Grudem writes. "In His great wisdom, God decided that he would not apply to us the benefits of Christ's redemptive work all at once." In this fallen world, "the last aspect . . . to be removed will be death."[27]

There is, therefore, a sense in which death is already defeated and a sense in which we still wait for the full benefits of the victory. Indeed, "the last enemy to be destroyed is death" (1 Cor. 15:26).

But Christ's defeat of death—demonstrated in His resurrection—is so *sure*, so *certain*, that the annihilation of death is an already-not-yet reality.

One writer compares death in its current state to a Canaanite king in the book of Judges who, having lost a battle with God's people, was allowed to continue ruling. But the victors had cut off his thumbs and big toes, parading him as a conquered foe

---

26. John 19:30; Revelation 1:18 NIV.
27. Grudem, *Systematic Theology*, 811, 810.

and preventing him from ever holding a sword or standing in battle again.[28]

This is how we picture the enemy of death in light of the work of Christ who, "having disarmed the powers and authorities [of death] . . . made a public spectacle of them, triumphing over them by the cross" (Col. 2:15 NIV).

Where does this leave us? Resting in Christ's victory—while also longing for its fullness to arrive. Some of the dearest passages in Scripture are those that whisper this promise over us, encouraging us to hold fast to the end, when "He will swallow up death forever; and the Lord GOD will wipe away tears from all faces" (Isa. 25:8). And, "He will wipe away every tear from their eyes, and death shall be no more, neither shall there be mourning, nor crying, nor pain anymore, for the former things have passed away" (Rev. 21:4).

And so we say with the final words of Scripture, *Maranatha*, "Come, Lord Jesus!" (Rev. 22:20).

In this book, we will continue to put flesh on these heady concepts. As we walk alongside others on the frontlines of facing death, may these truths take deep, steadying root in our own hearts too.

---

28. Juli Camarin, "Jesus Defeated Death & Made a Public Spectacle of It!—Colossians 2:15," Jcblog.net, April 18, 2014, https://www.jcblog.net/colossians/2/15-jesus-defeated-death-and-made-a-public-spectacle-of-it.

THREE

From the Sidelines

---

*Those who don't have the disease yearn deeply
to take it from their beloved—but they can't.
They can only watch.*[1]

—WALTER WANGERIN JR.

It was nearly Y2K—New Year's Eve, 1999—when Mom's hair began to fall out. A handful of my seventh-grade friends were staying over that night to ring in the new year. Together, we waited to see if the clocks would stop ticking, as some "experts" had predicted. My stepdad, whose birthday is January 1, always threw the best New Year's Eve parties—fireworks, feast, and all. Our house was the natural gathering place for all ages that night, even though Mom had started chemotherapy a few weeks before.

---

1. Walter Wangerin Jr., *Letters from the Land of Cancer* (Grand Rapids, MI: Zondervan, 2010), 30.

WE SHALL ALL BE CHANGED

Sleeping bags were strewn across the basement floor—some of my friends still asleep in them—when Mom came down the next morning, a fistful of chestnut-brown hair in her hand.

"I was brushing it before I got in the shower," she said, running her hands through her bouncy bob-length cut to demonstrate. Several strands clung to her fingers and joined the others in her palm. "It's coming out in clumps now."

That New Year's Day, she was crossing a threshold the doctors had told her to expect. Far from defeated, Mom seemed almost buoyant over this news, like she was checking something off a cancer to-do list. This disconnect between what she was saying and how she seemed to be receiving it—*great*, at least at first— would be a hallmark of Mom's cancer years and the cause of some of our biggest disagreements.

"New Year, new 'do," she quipped.

What better place for show-and-tell than a seventh-grade sleepover?

"Mom," I said after a too-long silence, feeling my friends watching, my eyes brimming with tears. "I'm so sorry."

I was trying, and failing, to take it as lightly as she seemed to be. I was nearly a teenager. Hair was everything. I had missed the bus more times than I could count trying to get a stubborn strand to curl at just the right angle under my chin. And here was my mom, losing hers.

I had already told my closest friends about Mom's cancer diagnosis by then. I had even wept over it publicly—albeit under the veil of darkness—as a "prayer request" around the campfire at our most recent middle school church retreat. There, and in the halls at school, it seemed to make me more mature, even cool, to be *going through something.* But the novelty of Mom's diagnosis wore off quickly when the cancer began to mar her appearance. When it became real.

First the hair, then the surgery, then the wig and the side effects. My mom had been in the best shape of her life at the time. She regularly ran 10K races and easily popped up on a single water ski behind the boat we took out on Kansas lakes, developing her tan all the while.

But, during treatments, her skin took on a ghostly pallor. She smelled like sanitized hospital sheets instead of Pantene Pro-V. On days she received chemo treatments, I would come home from school to find her lying very still in bed—willing herself to not get sick. Having lived with a mild case of Ménière's disease, an inner ear disorder that can cause dizzy spells and vomiting, Mom battled vertigo with a practiced determination.

I would gingerly perch on the opposite corner of her bed after coming home from school on those days, assessing whether a hug would throw off her equilibrium.

Even when Mom maintained miraculous composure, I felt off-balance in this new reality. I was learning to recognize the difference between good days and bad, the half-mouth smile she mustered for us to mask genuine discomfort and pain. I knew she wanted to protect my sister and me from this illness. But I also knew she couldn't, not completely.

IT'S NOT "ABOUT YOU," AND YET IT IS

One of the hardest aspects of facing the diagnosis or death of a loved one is that it's not about *us*—and yet it impacts us deeply.

My mom's wrestle with cancer was first and foremost *hers*. But it was also the primary trial in my stepdad's, my sister's, and my life for most of those years.

I remember the milestones of her disease alongside the milestones of my own life. Seven years after her initial diagnosis, Mom's cancer returned when I was a junior in college. Then, after a few years' respite, the cancer reared its head again while I was pregnant with my first child. It began to take over more and more of Mom's body as we were welcoming our second child and then our third. It never really retreated.

"How's your mom?" was a regular refrain among friends who had gotten to know us over a decade of adult life at our church in Virginia. As new members joined our home group, I struggled to explain the nuances when others asked for updates. "Well, the cancer has spread to her lungs and liver, but she's still as chipper as ever." "Oh us? We're fine. My mom has cancer, but she's had cancer for a long time."

Looking back, I see my mom's cancer story as a Venn diagram intersecting with my own and with others'. Each new development impacted us in ways that overlapped and diverged.

There were times in between Mom's visits that I gladly compartmentalized, talking and thinking about her cancer only as often as necessary and channeling my energy into an exhausting season with young children. There were times I went to counseling because I wasn't sure how to feel, times I needed spaces where I could be both grieving my mom's mortality and also, well, *mad at her* on occasion.

In the midst of her increasingly regular, somewhat consuming visits from her home in Kansas to our home in Virginia, I wondered how to find a sustainable rhythm for life with a job and young kids. How were we to pace ourselves and our grief when Mom may have only a year to live—or maybe many more?

Cancer wasn't some point-in-time trial for us to get through. It was the waters we swam in, the language we spoke, the backdrop to the highs and lows of the rest of our lives.

PERMISSION SLIP

It was my closest friends who gave me something I didn't know I needed as time marched on and Mom's cancer remained: permission to have my own process. They let this trial be not only about my mom, but also about me sometimes.

In case you need that same permission, let me extend it to you now: it's *okay* to have your own trial spinning off of the trial your loved one is experiencing. In fact, it's inevitable—even if you know others have it *worse*, even if you try to talk yourself out of how it's impacting you. Suffering isn't always relative. Sometimes it just is.

Maybe you're weary from the long stretch of caregiving and afraid to acknowledge it out loud. Maybe you have your own set of things you're grieving, your own surprising joys that pop up, and you don't know if there's room for them to exist. Your joys and sorrows may at times rise and fall in step with your loved one's—but they don't have to. God is not limited to managing one trial at a time; He can handle your emotions too.

The Bible gives us a similar permission slip in the face of sickness and death. It not only allows but also models lament in the face of loss. The dictionary definition of lament is "a passionate expression of grief or sorrow."[2] But I prefer a definition I'll paraphrase from Pastor Mark Vroegop, author of *Dark Clouds, Deep Mercy*.[3] Lament, he said in a sermon on Psalm 77, is the language of a people who believe in God's sovereignty, but live in the real world of tragedy.[4] If you have recently lost or faced a diagnosis with someone you love, this is a language you need.[5]

There are more psalms of lament than any other type in the Bible. They say, in one form or another, "This is not the way life was supposed to be!" But every lament is also a prayer of implausible faith. When we lament, we are turning *toward* God, rather than away. Our prayer then becomes a bold declaration of at least two truths: I am hurting, and You are a God who hears.

We can lament, then, even if the worst hasn't happened yet. And we can lament even if it has. We can grieve, even if we know our loved one is now "in a better place," as many like to assure us. Doing so does not reflect a lack of faith. Rather, "grief is existential testimony to the worth of the one loved," Nicholas Wolterstorff writes in *Lament for a Son*.[6]

The devout men who buried Stephen after he was publicly stoned to death also "made great lamentation over him" (Acts 8:2). They did this despite hearing Stephen testify to his own salva-

---

2. Oxford Languages, "Lament," Google dictionary search.

3. Mark Vroegop, *Dark Clouds, Deep Mercy: Discovering the Grace of Lament* (Wheaton, IL: Crossway, 2019).

4. Mark Vroegop, "The Grace of Lament," (sermon), Capitol Hill Baptist Church, September 8, 2019, https://www.capitolhillbaptist.org/sermon/the-grace-of-lament/.

5. And in the raw days of fresh loss, I encourage you to simply turn to the psalms of lament. If you need a soundtrack of modern lament, Bethany Barnard's "All My Questions" 2021 album is a beautiful choice.

6. Nicholas Wolterstorff, *Lament for a Son* (Grand Rapids, MI: Eerdmans, 1987), 5.

tion, saying "Lord Jesus, receive my spirit" as he was being stoned (Acts 7:59). They did not cry because they doubted whether Stephen's spirit had really been received by God.

No, "their sorrow showed the genuine grief that they felt at the loss of fellowship with someone whom they loved," Grudem writes, "and it was not wrong to express this sorrow—it was right."[7]

We have already mentioned the tears Jesus shed at the grave of Lazarus, a friend He would momentarily raise back to life (John 11:1–44). The God-man who took on flesh also let tears stream down His cheeks. He wept over the grief of the sisters before Him and, no doubt, over the existence of death at all in the world created and sustained by His own hands (Col. 3:17–18).

This shortest verse in the Bible—"Jesus wept" (John 11:35)—demonstrates a great deal about the God who sees our grief, even if it makes others uncomfortable. We do not need to talk ourselves out of emotions that even Jesus displayed. Before He conquered the very existence of death, He mourned it.

In a 2018 article, theologian Michael S. Horton commended Mary for bringing her full emotions to the Lord Jesus.[8] "Lord, if you had been here, my brother would not have died," she says after falling at His feet (John 11:32).

"Living in denial of tragedy, too many Christians live schizophrenic spiritual lives: outwardly smiling and brimming with trust

7. Wayne Grudem, *Systematic Theology: An Introduction to Biblical Doctrine* (Leicester, UK: Inter-Varsity Press, 1994), 814.

8. Michael S. Horton, "The Last Enemy and The Final Victory," September 1, 2018, modernreformation.org/resource-library/articles/the-last-enemy-and-the-final-victory/. The article originally appeared in the January/February 2005 issue of *Modern Reformation* under the title "Singing the Blues with Jesus."

and joy, but inwardly filled with doubts and anger," Horton writes. He says they would be better served to follow Mary's example and run to Christ. "Bring him your doubts, frustration, and even anger. He can handle it. Remember the cross and God-forsakenness of the Beloved: God, too, knows how to sing the blues."[9]

Paul also said he would have had "sorrow upon sorrow" if his friend Epaphroditus had died (Phil. 2:27). And he did not tell the Thessalonians in his letter to them that they should not grieve loved ones that have died in Christ. He said they should not grieve "*as others do who have no hope*" (1 Thess. 4:13).

How often has the phrase "grieve with hope!" been doled out as directions for Christians to cover up what they feel? But this hope we have in the face of grief is not to be applied like under-eye concealer. Rather, we must learn to live in the tension between the two. To grieve with hope is to place the full weight of our grief on one end of the scales of eternity—and to place our unbreakable hope on the other. It is to wait well for the eternal outweighing.

We can be assured until then that the Lord does not rush us but pauses to weep with us over loss, even the loss of those whose souls are swept into His presence: "Precious in the sight of the LORD is the death of his saints" (Ps. 116:15).

As a modern example, Wolterstorff beautifully grieves the loss of his twenty-five-year-old son to a mountain-climbing accident in his raw book, written in the year following his son's death. He did this even though his son Eric trusted in Christ.[10] Grieving

---

9. Horton, "The Last Enemy."

10. In a more recent book, pastor Tim Challies also grapples beautifully with God's sovereignty and goodness while reeling from the sudden loss of his son. Tim Challies,

with hope is still grief; hope does not diminish what he calls the "malevolence" of death.[11]

But it was "through the prism of [his] tears" that Wolterstorff, already a theologian and author, came to see and know his "suffering God" at close proximity.[12] For this reason, the author rails against other philosophies that try to rein in our lament when the Bible has no such interest.

"The stoics of antiquity said: Be calm. Disengage yourself. Neither laugh nor weep," Wolterstorff writes. But "Jesus says: Be open to the wounds of the world. Mourn humanity's mourning, weep over humanity's weeping, be wounded by humanity's wounds, be in agony over humanity's agony. But do so in the good cheer that a day of peace is coming."[13]

DRAW NEAR

One dictionary defines stoicism as "the endurance of pain or hardship without the display of feelings and without complaint."[14] It can be a powerful coping mechanism, promising to shield us from the very emotions we refuse to feel. But it can also be a stiff-arm to the presence of God. Stoicism may feel strong, but "weakness is the Spirit's womb," Paul E. Miller writes in his book *J-Curve*.[15]

Seasons of Sorrow: The Pain of Loss and the Comfort of God (Grand Rapids, MI: Zondervan, 2022).

11. Wolterstorff, *Lament for a Son*, 50.

12. Ibid., 81.

13. Ibid., 86.

14. Oxford Languages, "Stoicism," Google dictionary search.

15. Paul E. Miller, *J-Curve: Dying and Rising with Jesus in Everyday Life* (Wheaton, IL: Crossway, 2019), 31.

Rather, when we allow ourselves to feel the brokenness of these situations, of life in a fallen world, we also open ourselves to the care of the One who promises to be near to the broken-hearted and crushed in spirit (Ps. 34:18).

Just like ignoring death doesn't serve us, neither does pretending it doesn't impact us. If we don't acknowledge the fissures left by our loved one's diagnosis or death, we can't let others into them. And we can't let the Lord into them. What we don't acknowledge will not go away. Rather, it's likely to fester into a full-blown personal crisis (at inopportune moments, trust me).

When the loss does come, whether quickly or after many years of trudging toward it, some of us walk away with new titles to represent the cataclysmic shift that's taken place. Death makes us widows or widowers, grieving parents or parentless orphans. But what do we do with losses our culture tells us are somehow less severe, or at least less *named*? What do we do with losses that haven't yet arrived, when the grief over them is just as real as if they have?

We find people who can see *us* and our grief. We find places— *Lord, may the church be among them*—where people make space for it anyway. And we remember that, even if all others are sorry comforters, we serve a God who sees and who beckons us to come. The only qualification is being overwhelmed.

"Come to me, *all* you who are weary and burdened," Jesus is recorded saying in Matthew 11:28, "and I will give you rest" (NIV).

The invitation is not only for the newly diagnosed but also for those of us who are in the waiting room. It is not only for the sick and weary but also for those of us who thought we had it all together. It is not only for the weakening but also for those of us wondering how much longer we can "be strong."

In the wake of these tragedies, then, we grieve, we lament, and we come. We open our Bibles. We find solace in Lamentations and the psalms of lament, quietly wondering, "Have these always been in here?" When we are shaking and barely surviving, God is steady. We endure, living entire days on the manna of a song lyric that rings true or a Scripture passage memorized long ago that, suddenly, springs from the dust.

Months later, we realize the chest we've been beating on and wetting with our tears is that of the very One who promised to be with us in this. When the fog begins to lift, we see that the One who felt distant has been near all along.

Sometimes, writes Corrie ten Boom, reflecting on the first verse of Psalm 91, "when one is abiding under the shadow of the Almighty, there will be no light, but that is only because God's presence is so near."[16]

WHEN THE FOG LIFTS

Still, I wondered in the aftermath of my mom's eventual death, why is it that the preacher in Ecclesiastes says, "It is *better* to go to the house of mourning than to go to the house of feasting" (Eccl. 7:2)?

This thought comes to me as the pain of mourning stings anew

---

16. Corrie ten Boom, *Tramp for the Lord* (Old Tappan, NJ: Fleming H. Revell Company, 1974), 59. Reflecting on how her father read Psalm 91 to their family the night they were arrested for helping Jews escape Nazis in Holland during the Holocaust. This book is a sequel of sorts to *The Hiding Place* and depicts her travels as a Christian speaker after she was released from a concentration camp.

in a grocery store aisle when I come across my mom's favorite variety of onions—of all things. ("Remember to get Vidalias," I hear her telling me as she sends me to the store for guacamole ingredients. "They're the sweet ones.")

When I get home, I search online for the second half of the verse. Why is mourning better than ignoring? Why think about death at all? And the internet answers, "For this is the end of all mankind, and the living will lay it to heart" (Eccl. 7:2).

We should go to the house of mourning—rehearsing the truth of God-with-us as we go—because we *will* go to the house of mourning. We should go to the house of mourning because the sickness that's striking our loved ones has a way of striking us too.

Thinking about death—about a mom who was a phone call away one week and gone the next—became inevitable for me. Not only did I see death up close, but now death seemed to have followed me out into reality.

It was a robin's egg, shattered after falling from its nest, on my neighborhood walk. It was our beloved dog of nine years coming home from the vet with her own cancer diagnosis and months to live. It was scrawled across my daily Bible readings—*you shall surely die . . . and He died . . . the Son of Man has come . . . to give His life . . . and the old has passed away.* Had this theme always been there too?

Things I had seen a hundred times now seemed to fit squarely into these new buckets, this theology of death I was timidly carrying around. It felt like a burden at first. But it also gave me a category for so many aspects of a world that in its present form is passing away (1 Cor. 7:31). It gave me a place to put the pain. And it reminded me that God does not stand far off when I am honest about the ache.

> For thus says the One who is high and lifted up,
>> who inhabits eternity, whose name is Holy:
> I dwell in the high and holy place,
>> and also with him who is of a contrite and lowly spirit,
> to revive the spirit of the lowly,
>> and to revive the heart of the contrite. (Isa. 57:15)

FOUR

Fight or Flight

Death is a sort of lens, though I used
to think of it as a wall or a shut door.
It changes things and makes them clear.
Maybe it is the truest way of knowing
this dream, this brief and timeless life.[1]

—WENDELL BERRY, *HANNAH COULTER*

My mom hardly missed a day of work during her first go-round
with cancer at age forty-one. The day after an infusion of chemotherapy, she'd put on her wig, apply a little makeup—though she
never did get good at penciling in eyebrows where there were
none—and head back to the office where she worked as a banker.

"Your mom is the strongest woman I know," people would
say, "working through all those treatments."

For a few years, my mom's breast cancer story was indeed a
movement from strength to strength. It mirrored the ad campaigns

---

1. Wendell Berry, *Hannah Coulter* (Washington, DC: Shoemaker & Hoard, 2004), 157.

featuring women flexing their "cancer strong" arms beneath Rosie-the-Riveter bandanas. They ran 5Ks wearing bright pink "beat cancer" T-shirts (and some that put a different four-letter word in front of cancer). The local Christian nonprofit that gave teddy bears to women who had undergone breast cancer surgery was called Victory in the Valley, after all. Losing to cancer, it all seemed to imply, was not an option.

My mom's story was beginning to fit that narrative too. One day, after surgery and a few months of treatment, we got the tentative news that the cancer was gone. Conquered. Defeated. Overcome.

I don't remember celebrating, though, or feeling much certainty. I only recall the follow-up checks becoming less and less dreaded and less and less frequent—every three months, then every six months, then once a year. Mom's hair grew in salt-and-pepper spikes. When it was long enough for a bob, the lifelong brunette dyed it blonde.

"Why not?" she said.

Some people reserve their cancer-free celebrations for the seven-year mark, the day of jubilee when the medical community considers you statistically out of the woods for a recurrence. It was at that seven-year-mark appointment in October of 2007 that Mom got the news: the cancer was back.

I was a junior in college, crying in the back stairwell of my sorority house three hours from home when she told me. The cancer cropped up in a strip of chest muscle that, with the breast tissue long ago removed by mastectomy, had been holding an implant in place.

It's hard to remember what we knew then versus what we would come to understand. I have only my own memories to inform me now that Mom is no longer here. (She managed every detail of her medical care until her last week.) I remember knowing that this round with cancer would be different, that the stakes were higher, that the solutions would not be as tidy.

We couldn't have known then what it would mean for her cancer to never again come to a medical conclusion. Instead of victories, cancer became a series of semicolons with each recurrence or spread appearing more quickly than the one before. After small spots of cancer showed up in Mom's lung sack in 2014 and then in her liver the next year, the disease never again went away.

Cancer became for Mom what the metastatic breast cancer community now describes as a "chronic disease," one that constantly whispers of both the need to fight and of the seeming futility of it. It gets harder to use victorious language when the treatments that buy you more time are harder on your body than the cancer they're trying to kill.

Her cancer journal, where she jotted appointment dates, her latest laundry list of symptoms, and bloodwork results alongside prayers and praises is sprinkled with her signature phrases. "Piddledink!" meant that the results were not great. "Just in the nick of time! Thank you, Lord!!" meant she got her hands on a new drug. "What's next???" or "Well, here we go again!" meant the latest drug had stopped working.

But Mom had her motivations. With her initial diagnosis in 1999 came a promise she perhaps had no business making to her young daughters: "I will never stop fighting to be here with you." She repeated this promise as necessary over the years. It was understandable, her desire to give us a steady bit of earth to stand on when our reality was tilting beyond recognition. When my sister and I started having children, the reasons for "Grandma" to stick around at any cost only multiplied.

We're convinced she prayed and pushed and sheer-willed her way into each extra year with them and with us.

BUT EVEN IF

Is it wrong, I wonder now, for a Christian to ask for more time, to fight for it by any means necessary? Does it cause us to look for victory in a place where it isn't promised?

In 2 Kings 20, King Hezekiah faced a deadly illness of his own and asked God for more time. He turned his face to the wall—a picture of the new boundary line God had drawn on his life—and prayed to the One who could change it. God answered and granted him fifteen more years.

I don't know what that conversation between my mom and God looked like. Considering who she was, I imagine it looked more like Jacob's wrestling match with the Almighty than a quiet weeping in her bed.[2] I do know that, from diagnosis to dying day, God granted her twenty years.

---

2. Gen. 32:22–32.

Was it cowardly for Hezekiah to ask for more time? Or simple stubbornness for my mom to eke out extra years with the help of chemotherapy and countless clinical trials—life by the common grace of chemistry, as she liked to say? Would it have been holier or more obedient for them to say like the Savior, "Not my will, but yours, be done" (Luke 22:42)?

But Jesus Christ also prayed these words first: "Father, if you are willing, remove this cup from me" (v. 42). If Jesus asked for deliverance from imminent death, then surely, it's okay for us to ask for it too. It would be ignoring our human instinct of fighting death to do otherwise. But what do we do when the answer is no? Or yes, but only for a little while?

For those of us who pray in the face of diagnoses or imminent death, perhaps the example from Scripture most worth emulating is the one we find in chapter 3 of the book of Daniel.

Among those exiled to the Babylonian kingdom were three Jewish men—Shadrach, Meshach, and Abednego—who refused to bow down to a golden image of King Nebuchadnezzar. Furious, the king ordered that the men be thrown into a fiery furnace heated to seven times its usual temperature. "Then what god will be able to rescue you from my hand?" Nebuchadnezzar said, taunting them and their God (Dan. 3:15 NIV).

The three men told the king in response, "If we are thrown into the blazing furnace, the God we serve is able to deliver us from it, and he will deliver us from Your Majesty's hand. But even if he does not, we want you to know, Your Majesty, that we will not serve your gods or worship the image of gold you have set up" (Dan. 3:17–18 NIV).

You may know how the story ends—that the three men were miraculously delivered unharmed through the blaze, despite it being so hot that it killed the guards who threw them into it. That a fourth man, looking like "a son of the gods" was seen walking around in the fire with them. That Nebuchadnezzar marveled at their deliverer, the "Most High God," remarking that "no other god can save in this way" (Dan. 3:22–30 NIV).

But what I want us to take from this story as it relates to death is the "even if." At a moment when a king is daring to elevate himself above God—when the men given a death sentence could have justifiably said God's very reputation was on the line—they did not stake God's name on their salvation from death. Instead, they declared two things: that God was able to deliver them and that God did not have to.

What we proclaim when we borrow the words of these three men in the face of our own fiery trials is a faith that "is in God, not in healing," wrote Joseph Bayly, an American author who lost three of his seven children at young ages.[3]

To say *even if* "is an admission that we are fallible, that we may be wrong in our conviction that God will heal and thereby postpone death. (Death is always merely postponed.)," Bayly continues. And, to be clear, he adds that "death, not healing is the great deliverance from all pain and suffering."

Yet, when push comes to shove, many of us don't live like this is true.

One study found that terminally ill cancer patients who "drew

---

3. Joseph Bayly, *The View from a Hearse* (Bloomington, IN: Warhorn Media, 2014), 33, eBook.

comfort from religion" were three times more likely to seek aggressive, life-prolonging care in the week before they died than those who were less religious. Those who were religious were also far more likely to want doctors to "do everything possible" to keep them alive, the study found.[4]

It's like the 1965 Loretta Lynn song, "Everybody Wants to Go to Heaven," which also reminds us: no one likes dying to get there.[5] In the song, Lynn holds up as examples of this mantra both Hezekiah and Jesus asking for more time before repeating her conclusion—nobody really likes the going-through-death part.

IS IT WRONG TO FEAR DEATH?

Human beings are layered creatures, and we are full of ironies. Something deep inside us longs for more than this world offers. Yet our bodies and minds intuitively fight death, the mode of deliverance from this life to the next.

Scientists call it the "survival instinct," this phenomenon that keeps humans pursuing life-saving measures regardless of their outlook on the afterlife. Throw us in the ocean, and it causes us to swim. When the human brain senses danger, it signals stress hormones that prepare the body to either get away from the danger (flight) or dig in for battle (fight).

---

4. A. C. Phelps et al., "Religious Coping and Use of Intensive Life-Prolonging Care Near Death in Patients with Advanced Cancer," *The Journal of the American Medical Association* (2009): https://pubmed.ncbi.nlm.nih.gov/19293414/.

5. I only know of this song because the David Crowder Band covered it, opening their 2005 album by repeating this intriguing chorus line. David Crowder and bandmember Michael Hogan also wrote a book titled *Everybody Wants to Go to Heaven, But Nobody Wants to Die* (Grand Rapids, MI: Zondervan, 2009).

Today, we read about the harmful underside of these survival instincts from places like the American Institute of Stress. In an age in which few Americans are chased by actual lions or bears, "any perceived threat, whether physical or emotional, real or imaginary" can kick our bodies' survival instincts into high gear. When our minds overreact to these threats, our systems get flooded with "excessive hormones that can be harmful to our health."[6]

Christians suffer from many of these same symptoms of life in a fallen world, plagued by traffic jams and technology failures. And, when it comes to facing actual death, we can be just as tempted to turn to pop psychology and coping mechanisms. Some of that can be helpful. But, for those who trust in Christ, the greater reality that swallows up our primal fear of death is not meditation apps or mentally "manifesting" a better future. It is this: our God didn't just take on the *perception* of danger in death. He took on death itself. And Christ carries in His resurrected body the scars of His victory over death. He also bears with us the weight that remains.

"Surely he has borne our griefs and carried our sorrows," Isaiah prophesied of the suffering servant who would be "pierced for our transgressions" and "crushed for our iniquities" (Isa. 53:4-5).

On His body "the LORD has laid . . . the iniquity of us all" (Isa. 53:6).

Our Savior not only faced death. He put on flesh for that express purpose. He came down to die: "Being found in human

---

6. The American Institute of Stress, "21st Century Survival Instinct," February 24, 2020, https://www.stress.org/21st-century-survival-instinct.

form, he humbled himself by becoming obedient to the point of death, even death on a cross" (Phil. 2:8).

Perhaps the greatest comfort Christians have in the face of death, then, is that their God went first. Scripture calls the incarnate Christ "the pioneer" of our salvation who was made perfect through what He suffered—namely the bearing of sins through death on the cross.[7]

Jesus went first through death. And here's the astonishing result: He shared in our humanity and died in our humanity "so that by his death he might break the power of him who holds the power of death—that is, the devil." Why does He do this? To "free those who all their lives were held in slavery *by their fear of death*" (Heb. 2:14–15 NIV).

This passage does not say that Christians should no longer fear death. Rather, it says that Christians need no longer be enslaved by the fear of death. Jesus went through death to break its grip of bondage on us in this life.

As Billings writes, "The goal for the Christian life is not eliminating the fear of death but removing death from its throne. For as long as the fear of death rules, we cannot fully serve, worship, and bear witness to the true King, Jesus."[8]

---

7. Hebrews 2:10 NIV.
8. J. Todd Billings, *The End of the Christian Life: How Embracing Our Mortality Frees Us to Truly Live* (Grand Rapids, MI: Brazos Press, 2020), 76.

NOT YOUR LIFE, BUT THEIRS

Perhaps you've thought about how you'd feel if you were the one to get the dreaded diagnosis or call, to reason that you'd embrace it all as nobly as Job did (at least, at first): "The LORD gave, and the LORD hath taken away," you'd say, head held high. "Blessed be the name of the LORD."[9]

But once we've walked with others through sickness and death, we know it's never quite that simple—not even for Christians. For the Christian, death is a paradox. It is a great enemy of all the life we currently know. And it is sweet deliverance from all that is hard in this life into the very presence of God. The apostle Paul grapples with this dilemma in his letter to the Philippians, concluding that both options have their benefits: "to live is Christ, and to die is gain."[10] He continues:

> If I am to live in the flesh, that means fruitful labor for me. Yet which I shall choose I cannot tell. I am hard pressed between the two. My desire is to depart and be with Christ, for that is far better. But to remain in the flesh is more necessary on your account. (Phil. 1:22–24)

It is one thing to hold your own life loosely like Paul, to see evenhandedly the trade-offs between remaining in a sin-soaked world and going to the next. But it is another to watch a loved one have this decision made for them.

---

9. Job 1:21 KJV.
10. Philippians 1:21.

In his book *Letters from the Land of Cancer*, Walter Wangerin Jr. wrote that despite the harrowing treatments plaguing his body, his sickness was in many ways harder on his wife, Thanne, than on him.

"Her waiting and the weight upon her shoulders outreaches mine," he observed. "And those who don't have the disease yearn deeply to take it from their beloved—but they can't. They can only watch."[11]

What's perhaps hardest as a bystander witnessing someone else's decline is to know where things actually stand medically. When healing seems out of reach, what can still hold your hope?

Hoping at all can become a heavy burden when the trial outstays its welcome. Mere acquaintances don't stick around for this part. They don't hear of the symptoms stacking one on another, and they don't witness the pain as this happens. They pray, but from a distance. The lowest points—when the smile fades and the only hope left is that which the co-sufferers can still bear to carry—these are reserved for the ones who love from eye-level.

WHAT TO HOPE FOR

When death comes to the door, it has a way of revealing what our hope is truly in and promptly disposing of lesser versions. If we have eyes only for earthly healing, that hope can quickly be dashed on the rocks of an untimely demise or a long, chaotic ordeal.

Yes, God can heal, and yes, Christ healed during His earthly

---

11. Walter Wangerin Jr., *Letters from the Land of Cancer* (Grand Rapids, MI: Zondervan, 2010), 29–30.

ministry. We pray for it and invite others to pray too. We plumb the depths of medical interventions. We beg for more years.

But though He healed some, Jesus didn't even come close to healing all the lepers that longed for it in His day. Even the man He raised from the dead did not live forever. Such physical healing was an important aspect of Christ's ministry—an arrow pointing to the fuller reality of the resurrection to come—but it does not appear to have been the focus.

Christians can and should pray for the terminally ill, Bayly writes, but "what happens if the prayer for healing is based on belief that God's promise to heal is unconditional, that lack of faith alone can circumvent healing?" The sad outcome, he writes, is that "life's final months are turned into playacting instead of a mature, deepening experience with God and loved ones . . . Heaven recedes as a symbol of hope, and the man of faith looks to continuation of life on earth as the zenith of his desire no less than does the man of no faith."

In summary, Bayly writes, "Death becomes faith's defeat instead of heaven's door."[12]

It bears repeating: "If in Christ we have hope in this life only, we are of all people most to be pitied" (1 Cor. 15:19).

When death rears its head around us and in us and our theology buckles under its weight, we can turn to lesser hopes. We can hope for healing alone, at all costs, squelching the hope held out by a resurrected Savior. We can try to ignore it, choosing instead to be laser-focused on the good that remains. We can sink our

---

12. Bayly, *The View from a Hearse*, 32.

teeth into a sugary-sweet theology that prefers to place a positive spin on hardship, whether ours or others', as if God's very name is in jeopardy if we say out loud how much it hurts.

But each of these misses the mark of holding two things in tension: God's eternal goodness and our present pain.

In the thick of it, these realities feel magnetically opposed. It feels impossible to comprehend how they could ever fit into the same worldview. Forcing them, for now, will not do. Job's friends tried to explain them away, and so will many others. But those who are suffering must sit with them. We must let them exist in separate hands for a while, refusing to let go of either God's goodness or our pain, running our fingers over the contours of each. We groan, "How long?" We pray, "Thy will be done." We whisper, "Even if you don't."

Sometimes in our pain we are tempted to give up on the goodness of God, to throw it away like a childish idea that doesn't fit the form of adult realities. We are equally tempted to assent to the goodness of God while whitewashing our suffering to make it fit the picture we want to portray. We want to be done with the pain anyway, so we cover it up with *God-works-all-things-together-for-good* platitudes. Rather than facing and lamenting the pain, we distill the promises of Scripture down to coffee-mug mantras that are easier to hold on to.

But if we learn to sit with the heaviness of these truths—if we let them feel in opposition yet hold them both anyway—we find that the weight shapes us over time. The full acknowledgement of each produces in us the sort of endurance that Romans 5:3–5 says leads to character—and to a hope that does not put us to shame. A hope that can live, flourish even, in the midst of our *even if*.

LOOKING IT IN THE EYE

There is a scene in the 1990 Disney film *The Rescuers Down Under* when the characteristically scared mouse, Bernard—desperate to save his beloved Bianca and the young boy—works up the courage to face a snoring wild hog. This tiny mouse, clearly terrified, grabs the slumbering beast by the horns on the front of his snout, and after mumbling an "Excuse me," says this: "Now look, I've got a long way to go. You're . . . gonna take me there, and you're not gonna give me any trouble about it, right?"[13] The pig squeals in submission and off they go.

That illustration is a little too triumphant, perhaps. But I see something familiar in it: Bernard's greatest fear, when fully faced, becomes the way of his deliverance. He didn't come to this conclusion on his own. It was so counterintuitive that a mouse could tame a wild beast that Bernard might not have believed it had he not seen their fearless guide-mouse ride up on a rattlesnake earlier in the story.

As Christians, we know that if Christ tarries, death will be the mode of our deliverance from this sin-soaked world and into His very presence. We do not *welcome* it because of this. But, because of this, *we can look it in the eye*. We can grab death by the horns and say, "How then shall I live?" We can tell one another stories of our own days facing death, whether we stare it down ourselves or walk with others toward it.

---

13. Hendel Butoy and Mike Gabriel, directors. *The Rescuers Down Under,* 1990, Walt Disney Pictures, Disney Plus.

I picture Paul doing just that when he writes to the believers in Philippi, "I want to know Christ—yes, to know the power of his resurrection and participation in his sufferings, *becoming like him in his death*, and so, somehow, attaining to the resurrection from the dead" (Phil. 3:10–11 NIV).

Paul is touching on this mystery of the Christian life, the upside-down nature of the kingdom to which we belong. If our King was crowned on a cross, then perhaps victory in this life doesn't look like we think it should. The Christian life itself is a type of dying. We are to die to this world, to take up our cross, and lose our life for the sake of Christ.[14] We don't just remember Good Friday and Resurrection Sunday. We live cruciform in their wake. We see that the way down must come before the way up.[15]

Walking with others through sickness and death is an opportunity to try on these realities, to rehearse a hope that lives in the face of death because it anticipates deliverance through it.

I thought for many years that my mom wasn't willing to accept "losing her battle" with cancer. If she was, she rarely spoke about it with us, the daughters to whom she swore she would "never stop fighting to live."

But, after she died, I found her version of an "even if" prayer penned in her journal before her last major medical appointment. The news would not be good that day, and somehow she had been made ready to receive it either way: "Here we are at the

---

14. Galatians 6:14; Matthew 6:24–25.

15. Paul Miller's book *J-Curve: Dying and Rising with Jesus in Everyday Life* (Wheaton, IL: Crossway, 2019) helpfully expounds on this concept.

cliff, waiting to find out if there's a bridge to here or a bridge to you, Jesus. Help me to walk this next chapter—long or short—with grace and faith beyond my feeble belief."

FIVE

Our Fading Frames

My flesh and my heart may fail,
but God is the strength of my heart
and my portion forever.

—PSALM 73:26

I remember the way lake water left a sheen on my mom's skin. Driving around in a boat with an engine too loud for conversation gave us little else to do than stare at the graying water, the cotton-candy clouds, and our knees propped up on the engine cover in front of us.

I can still feel the parched sensation of my own skin, blow-dried by the hot wind and chalk-dusted with layers of sunscreen. All summer long, my skin alternated in shade between very pale and sunburned, depending on how wise I had been on a given day. But this same unrelenting sun turned my mom's outermost layer into light-brown leather. Her golden color came back quickly each summer, a holdover from a youth spent almost entirely in or on the water—and some mix of genes I did not inherit.

Children don't mean to pay attention to their mothers' arms, legs, feet, and hands. They just do. It was second nature for me to watch the hands and knees that had shown me how to shave and how to glide over choppy Kansas waters on a slalom ski.

My mom hardly ever held still long enough for this sort of accidental study. But long boat drives back from a day of skiing, swimming, and sandwich-making left her placid, like the still surface of those tree-lined Missouri lakes we visited only on vacation. Her hands would rest in her lap, fingers finally relaxed. Sometimes she'd even lean her head back and close her eyes under the engine-roar lullaby.

I may not remember many of the ancestry facts Mom dredged up in her later years, but I remember her skin. It is a map in my mind telling the story of her life as it evolved over time.

Later, it was the first part of her body to bear the marks of cancer treatment. I remember one chemotherapy drug that took a particular toll on the flesh of her hands and feet. This medicine somehow managed to spare the hair, leaving her blonde bob intact for a time, while pooling instead at the end of her extremities. There, it wreaked havoc on the quickly-dividing skin cells, turning her palms puffy, raw, and red. They peeled so badly that the lifelong banker joked about robbing a few financial institutions now that her fingerprints had nearly disappeared.

But still, the peeling and pain didn't stop her. When I was expecting my first daughter during the peak of these treatments in 2014, Mom came to Virginia to help me finish the nursery anyway. After an August day spent sanding and painting a dresser for the baby's room, I saw how the work rendered her hands even more beet red and sore.

"Oh, it's fine," she'd say. "Worth it to be here," she'd say. Later, though, she'd let us do the dishes, wincing as she rubbed thick lotion into her palms and knuckles.

Our bodies often tell us stories we'd rather not hear. This was especially true of my mom, who endured more than most bodies can handle during countless clinical trials ("a real guinea pig," she'd say). It wasn't until I read her cancer notebook after she died that I realized how constantly she played whac-a-mole with bodily symptoms, beating back one only to be waylaid by another.

What hope is there for those who endure like this, I wonder now, in bodies that once flourished but now falter and suffer?

I was in the midst of my own invincibility years—when the adolescent brain cannot conceive of its own immortality[1]— when my mom was first facing hers head on. But, by the work of God's Spirit in my little middle-school heart, I also felt flashes of

---

1. The female brain's frontal lobes do not complete the myelination process that insulates neurons until age twenty-five. Male brains don't reach this milestone that is associated with proper risk assessment, among other virtues, until age thirty. "When your frontal lobes finally complete their process of myelination, they begin to work properly and you stop doing dangerous things. Most importantly, you stop feeling immortal." Gary Wenk, PhD, "Why Do Teenagers Feel Immortal?," *Psychology Today,* August 23, 2010, https://www.psychologytoday.com/us/blog/your-brain-food/201008/why-do-teenagers-feel-immortal.

deep empathy toward her. During one, I penned the following verses onto her bathroom mirror with a dry-erase marker:

> Therefore we do not lose heart. Though outwardly we are wasting away, yet inwardly we are being renewed day by day. For our light and momentary troubles are achieving for us an eternal glory that far outweighs them all. So we fix our eyes not on what is seen, but on what is unseen, since what is seen is temporary, but what is unseen is eternal. (2 Cor. 4:16–18 NIV)

I remember how this verse stuck in my teenage head, scolding me when I spent too long in front of the mirror, fixated on the temporal. But mostly, I remember how weighty and necessary it felt in light of what my mom was enduring. She needed and *I needed* to know that these bodily troubles that felt anything but light will become so—once balanced by the eternal weight of glory.[2] As Paul wrote:

> For we know that if the earthly tent we live in is destroyed, we have a building from God, an eternal house in heaven, not built by human hands. Meanwhile we groan, longing to be clothed instead with our heavenly dwelling . . . so that what is mortal may be swallowed up by life. (2 Cor. 5:1–4 NIV)

EMBODYING THE GOSPEL

Our bodies carry in them reminders that we will not live forever. This is as true of those who have been given a terminal diagnosis

---

2. "For this light momentary affliction is preparing for us an eternal weight of glory beyond all comparison" (2 Cor. 4:17).

as it is of those who have not. The skin that dimples fresh and dewy around a toddler's chubby knuckles eventually flattens and freckles. In old age, it grows thin and papery, like tissue paper that barely conceals the blue veins still pumping beneath the surface.

The Bible, unlike the advertising industry, does not shy away from this reality. It compares our bodies to pop-up tents and to jars of clay—the reusable Tupperware equivalents of the ancient world. Scripture says we inhabit "bodies of death" that are weak and perishable.[3]

Yet, illogically, our bodies are also called "[temples] of the Holy Spirit" (1 Cor. 6:19) and "fearfully and wonderfully made," knit together by a careful Creator in our mothers' wombs (Ps. 139:14).

In our bodies, then, we carry all the beautiful and terrible tensions of the gospel. Remembering this gives us categories for the painful parts of being embodied—and lends us a greater vision for their redemption.

The first body was formed when God breathed life into dust, making humans the climax of a creation that He called "very good." Then the fall ushered frustration, futility,[4] and death into every aspect of that creation, including our bodies and the work they were made to do. When our frames are fading and frail, this is the part of the story they tell: "For you are dust, and to dust you shall return."[5]

It's a story that could end there. But it didn't. When the fullness

---

3. "Body of death" (Rom. 7:24), "weak" (Matt. 26:41), "perishable" (1 Cor. 15:53).

4. "For the creation was subjected to futility, not willingly, but because of him who subjected it, in hope that the creation itself will be set free from its bondage to corruption" (Rom. 8:20–21).

5. See Genesis chapters 2 and 3. Quote from Genesis 3:19.

of time had come, the story burst into living color.[6] "The Word became flesh and dwelt among us" (John 1:14). The very God through whom all things were made robed Himself in frail humanity.[7] The One who made us in God's image, *imago Dei*, took on a nature like ours to become God with us, *Immanuel*.

"Trace him, Christian," Charles Spurgeon once preached "He has left thee his manger to show thee how God came down to man.... Trace him along his weary way, as the Man of Sorrows, and acquainted with grief."[8]

Our God took on a body. Jesus Christ grew from infancy to manhood in a temporary tent like yours and mine. He who said "If I were hungry, I would not tell you, for the world and its fullness are mine" (Ps. 50:12) submitted Himself to basic bodily needs for food, clothing, and rest. Being embodied allowed Jesus to be "tempted as we are, yet without sin" (Heb. 4:15). Living the perfect life, which only He could do, made His body the spotless sacrifice for the sins of us all.[9]

In this way, Christ's embodiment lights the way for the redemption of our own: *You whose body has been broken by the sins of others, you who suffer from chronic illness, you who struggle to receive the*

---

6. "But when the fullness of time had come, God sent forth his Son, born of woman, born under the law, to redeem those who were under the law, so that we might receive adoption as sons" (Gal. 4:4–5).

7. "Robed in frail humanity" phrase from Matt Papa, Matt Boswell, Michael Bleecker in the hymn, "Come Behold the Wondrous Mystery" (Love Your Enemies Publishing, 2013).

8. From the sermon "The Condescension of Christ" on 2 Corinthians 8:9, September 13, 1857, The Spurgeon Center, https://www.spurgeon.org/resource-library/sermons/the-condescension-of-christ/#flipbook/.

9. "Knowing that you were ransomed from the futile ways inherited from your forefathers, not with perishable things such as silver or gold, but with the precious blood of Christ, like that of a lamb without blemish or spot" (1 Peter 1:18–19).

wrinkles and the wear-and-tear, "fix [y]our eyes on Jesus, the author and perfector of our faith, who for the joy set before Him endured the cross, scorning its shame, and sat down at the right hand of the throne of God" (Heb. 12:2 BSB). What ailment befalls you? What would change if you could lift your eyes *not* to a God who stands far off but to a Savior who stooped to suffer?

"Consider Him who endured [*in His body*] such hostility from sinners, so that you will not grow weary [*in your body*] and lose heart. In your struggle against sin, you have not yet resisted to the point of shedding your blood" (Heb. 12:3–4 BSB).[10]

When we lift our eyes to finally face our dust-to-dust existence, we can also see the bright-red trickle of blood flowing through it. Watch as it wells up into a life-giving stream. "Behold," Isaiah 43:19 foretold, "I am doing a new thing; now it springs forth, do you not perceive it? I will make a way in the wilderness and rivers in the desert." When our bodies fail us, this is the Savior to whom we look, the One from whose body—for us—blood and water flowed.[11]

But He's also the One whose sacrifice was so sufficient that He did not stay dead. In Christ, we see the way—through the death of the bodies we now know—to the resurrection life we can hardly imagine. In His resurrected body, we find the certain hope of our own bodily resurrection.

"Just as we have borne the image of the man of dust," 1 Corinthians 15 tells us, "we shall also bear the image of the man of

---

10. Additions in brackets are mine.

11. "But when they came to Jesus and saw that He was already dead, they did not break His legs. Instead, one of the soldiers pierced His side with a spear, and immediately blood and water flowed out" (John 19:33–34 BSB).

heaven" (v. 49). The Savior whose return we await "will transform our lowly body to be like his glorious body, by the power that enables him even to subject all things to himself" (Phil. 3:21).

This, Paul tells us, is a mystery. Wondrously, we shall all be changed.[12] He devotes almost all of chapter 15 of 1 Corinthians to exploring what this resurrection reality means for the bodies of those who trust in Christ. But how do you explain to someone who's never seen an oak tree what can come from a humble acorn? How do you describe a golden field of Kansas wheat to someone who has only held a kernel in his hand? "So it is with the resurrection of the dead," Paul writes. "What is sown is perishable; what is raised is imperishable.... It is sown in weakness; it is raised in power" (1 Cor. 15:42–43).

I will not be able to fully illuminate here what Paul, who encountered the resurrected Christ on the road to Damascus,[13] struggled to explain. Somehow, "the old body will become a new body. But it will still be your body. There will be continuity. God is able to do what we cannot imagine."[14]

ON BEING IN A BODY NOW

But what does all this mean when I am facing the frailties of my own body or the fading of a loved one's? It means, first and foremost, that our bodies matter. They and their failings are not an

---

12. 1 Corinthians 15:51.

13. See Paul's conversion on the road to Damascus in Acts 9. And, in 1 Corinthians 9:1, Paul's rhetorical questions "Have I not seen Jesus our Lord?"

14. John Piper, *The Purifying Power of Living by Faith in Future Grace* (Colorado Springs: Multnomah Books, 2005), 372.

afterthought to our Creator. What He made good and allows for a little while to be broken by sin, He will one day redeem. We carry in our feeble, broken shells the promise and potential of this glory.

This is why it aches all the more when our bodies and the bodies of those we love break down, whether slowly or suddenly.

"Ultimately the pains and struggles we experience in our bodies are not a sign that our bodies have no value," writes Sam Allberry in *What God Has to Say about Our Bodies*,[15] "but that God hasn't finished with them yet."

The Christian believes our bodies are not just throwaway packaging for our souls; these frames are part of the whole of us that will find their consummation in eternity. What we think about our bodies—and about God when our bodies suffer—has immense spiritual implications.

Before my mom's diagnosis, I paid little mind to death, sickness, or injury. The only serious ache I remember having, besides getting my wisdom teeth removed, was overstretching a ligament before a before a sporting event (okay, it was *cheerleading*). There was a *pop-pop* feeling, followed by an ice pack. But, within a few weeks, I was back to high kicking.

That sort of near-instant healing isn't as common in my mid-thirties. I now have regular migraines, mood swings, and a little early arthritis in my left knee to help keep my sense of infinitude in check. But what has changed my outlook on bodily shortcomings more than any of these was losing someone I loved. With

15. Sam Allberry, *What God Has to Say about Our Bodies: How the Gospel is Good News for Our Physical Selves* (Wheaton, IL: Crossway, 2021), 91.

my mom's death, the invincibility bubble of my earlier years went *pop-pop* too, and I'm afraid it won't recover. In fact, I'm glad it won't recover, because it wasn't very true.

When bodies fail, we can respond in a handful of ways.

In the absence of a greater story to tell ourselves about these frames, we can think too little of them and fail to heed what they're telling us. Both the pleasure-seeker and the pleasure-denier can be prone to this way of thinking. By abstaining from the physical joys of this world, the ascetic sees the body as merely in the way of the soul's progress. By indulging in all pleasures, meanwhile, the hedonist thinks such outward behavior will have little impact on the "true self." Both extremes fall short.

Christians, on the other hand, can easily be tempted to put too much emphasis on physical healing, placing all hope in a right-now redemption. As we discussed in chapter 4, such misplaced faith can lead to devastation. God *has*, *does*, and *is able to* heal from sickness and disease. But He does not promise to. The sin that stains every bit of creation plagues each of our bodies too. And there is no measure of faith that exempts a believer from this same state of fallenness.

The implication that someone is sick because they did something wrong—whether they did not have enough faith to guarantee their healing or did not use the right mix of essential oils to outsmart illness—is all too common in some faith communities. Allberry points out that Jesus is as unequivocally opposed to this way of thinking today as He was when He walked the earth. In the case of the blind man who it was assumed had sinned or inherited sin to become so, Jesus strongly corrected their assumptions: "It was not that this man sinned, or his parents" (John 9:3).

"The main connection between suffering and sin is at a general, humanity-wide level rather than at an individual level," Allberry writes. "It is not that one person's suffering is a sign of his or her sin, but that *anyone's* suffering is a sign of *everyone's* sin."[16]

I find this framework so helpful. It guards us from the lie that perfect wellness is something God offers only to those willing to internet-search their way into it. Our bodies are wonderfully made in the image of God. Our bodies are terribly broken because of the fall. Both can be true. And, taken together, they lead us to steward our bodies well while letting them point us to a fuller reality.

What if our longings for these bodies to do more, be more, and last longer are reminders that they were indeed made for more? In this light, the fading and frailty of our flesh is not pointless cruelty. Every wrinkle, every limp, every cancer cell can be both the result of sin *and* a gracious reminder.

We can take heart, then, not because our bodies are ultimate, but because, ultimately, they are signposts to somewhere. They point us to an embodied God who made a way for our temporary reality to be swallowed up by something greater. When our bodies falter and fail us, we are reminded to fix our hope to a firmer foundation. Then we can proclaim what Job did, even (and especially) in the midst of bodily anguish:

> For I know that my Redeemer lives,
>   and at the last he will stand upon the earth.

---

16. Allberry, *What God Has to Say about Our Bodies*, 93.

And after my skin has been thus destroyed,

yet in my flesh I shall see God. (Job 19:25–26)

BODILY SUFFERING

If God intends to resurrect us, then why doesn't He just do it now? Why does He allow us to linger under the curse for the rest of our lives? What does bodily suffering even accomplish in us?

These are the questions I imagine our bodies ask when, as the Bible describes it, they *groan* to be clothed and redeemed.[17] Even once we accept on some level that we must wait, we find a new question welling up within us, reflected in the Psalms: "How long, O LORD?" (Ps. 13:1).

Rather than snatching us up to heaven when we become Christians, God uses even fading bodies and death to accomplish His purposes in us, writes Grudem.[18] Death is not just the waters that, until Christ's return, we must pass through to get to eternity with God. Death is also the very process that makes us *ready* to be with God.

Grudem describes suffering and death as completing our union with Christ. Through death, we "imitate Christ in what he did,"[19] drawing near to Him both literally and metaphorically as we loosen our grip on all that kept us at a distance. Suffering and death were not just the way that Jesus took. They are the path to

---

17. Romans 8:23; 2 Corinthians 5:1–4.
18. Wayne Grudem, *Systematic Theology: An Introduction to Biblical Doctrine* (Leicester, UK: InterVarsity Press, 1994), 812.
19. Ibid.

true oneness with Christ for all who follow Him.

"Christ also suffered for you, leaving you an example, that you should follow in His footsteps" (1 Peter 2:21 BSB). Peter also writes that the goal is to "share Christ's sufferings, that you may also rejoice and be glad when his glory is revealed" (1 Peter 4:13).

For this reason, Paul grapples with whether it would be better to go ahead and draw nearer to Christ by going through death than to remain on earth, "*that I may know him* and the power of his resurrection, and *may share his sufferings*, becoming like him in his death" (Phil. 3:10).

This does not mean that suffering and death are endpoints we opt for any sooner than necessary. As death nears, we hold in delicate tension the sanctity of mortal life and a rising hope of eternal life in Christ.[20] But it does mean that God intends to use every scrap of pain to make us more like Him, to make us ready for His very presence.

Bodily suffering, whether terminal or temporary—perhaps more than any other worldly phenomenon—leaves us longing for a future when God is described as redeeming the brokenness of our bodies with the gentle stroke of a finger. Then, He "will wipe away every tear from [our] eyes, and death shall be no more, neither shall there be mourning, nor crying, nor pain anymore" (Rev. 21:4).

Until then, these aches and pains, these mortal diagnoses, remind us that this world—with all its thorns and thistles—is not our home. But because our God died in the flesh and lived

---

20. For more on this tension and how to practically make decisions for loved ones nearing death, consider former critical-care doctor Kathryn Butler's book *Between Life and Death: A Gospel-Centered Guide to End-of-Life Medical Care* (Wheaton, IL: Crossway, 2019).

to tell about it, we carry treasure in these jars of clay. Underneath the surface of our bodies and their limitations is the reminder that there is more to come.

As missionary Amy Carmichael movingly wrote of our embodied Savior:

> We follow a scarred Captain;
>> Should we not have scars?
> Under His faultless orders
>> We follow to the wars
> Lest we forget, Lord, when we meet,
>> Show us Thy hands and feet.[21]

---

21. Amy Carmichael, "Royal Scars," *Mountain Breezes: The Collected Poems of Amy Carmichael* (Fort Washington, PA: CLC Publications, 1999), 173.

SIX

On Birth
and Death

In every arrival there is a leavetaking;
in each one's growing up there is a growing old;
in every smile there is a tear;
in every success there is a loss.[1]

—HENRI NOUWEN, *A SORROW SHARED*

Never did I fight with my mother as I did in the days before becoming one myself.

I had resolved to deliver my first child as "naturally" as possible. So, though her due date had come and gone—Labor Day
really *would* have been a good time to go into labor—I was insist-
ing on waiting.

Had I known just how long I would wait, I would not have
invited my mom to fly out to Virginia to stare at me for twelve

---

1. Henri Nouwen, *A Sorrow Shared: A Combined Edition of the Nouwen Classics In Memo-
riam and A Letter of Consolation,* (Notre Dame, IN: Ave Maria Press, 2010), 77.

painstaking days. But there she was, asking me every time my stomach growled, "Was that a contraction?!" And there I was, taking long, escapist walks with the dog, bouncing endlessly on a yoga ball and journaling pages upon pages of prayers for God to "please (and without intervention)" start the labor that would deliver this baby into my arms.

My mom, meanwhile, was praying that I would stop being so stubborn and just have labor induced, or get a C-section, like she did.

Mom did not deliver by Cesarean because she elected to, but because a doctor in the late 1980s told her that her body, after hours of trying, "wasn't built for pushing out babies." Mom's thoughts on birth were also shaped by the agony of loss. In the years before I was born, she delivered a daughter who would not live outside the womb. Now that I've been a mother for a handful of years, I see that the thought of my having any unpredictable complications in a delivery room was more than she could bear.

But my husband and I had recently completed a class on the Bradley Method of Natural Childbirth—and we had the printed-out birth plan to show for it. C-section rates in the country had climbed since I was born but had been falling out of favor for about five years, from a peak in 2009.[2] The Bradley class also taught us to be skeptical of any and all interventions. I was determined to try things my way.

The end result was something of a compromise. I was giving birth on a military base since my husband was still active duty.

---

2. Clarel Antoine and Bruce K. Young, "Cesarean Section One Hundred Years 1920–2020: The Good, the Bad and the Ugly," *Journal of Perinatal Medicine* 49, no. 1 (2020): doi.org/10.1515/jpm-2020-0305.

And the friend-of-a-friend resident doctor I had convinced to let me wait for labor to arrive on its own told me after forty-one weeks and five days that it was time for the baby to be evicted. As terrified as I was of Pitocin, a synthetic oxytocin that causes and strengthens contractions (and, according to the Bradley teacher, signals the end of one's beloved birth plans), I only needed a little nudge of it before my body took over. That evening, our daughter Cora was born.

Much to my mom's surprise—and, honestly, my own—I delivered without pain medication. Part of me thinks I did it just to prove Mom wrong. But it also felt at the time like something I needed to prove to myself, a personal rite of passage into motherhood. I had never played with baby dolls or felt particularly maternal. I needed to feel myself becoming this other person, the mother this baby needed me to be. What surprised me, though, was how deeply and desperately I experienced not *my own* strength during birth, but the ever-present help of a God who goes by the name Deliverer.[3]

That is the name I would have written across the Ebenezer stone of Cora's arrival. Like Hagar proclaiming in the midst of her pain that God is the One who sees,[4] I have seen in the midst of mine that He delivers us through circumstances we cannot control.

BOOKENDS OF LIFE

"When a woman is giving birth, she has sorrow because her hour has come, but when she has delivered the baby, she no longer

---

3. "You are my help and my deliverer; O LORD, do not delay!" (Psalm 70:5b).
4. "So Hagar gave this name to the LORD who had spoken to her: "You are the God who sees me" (Gen. 16:13 BSB).

remembers the anguish, for joy that a human being has been born into the world" (John 16:21).

Since Cora was born, I have given birth to two more children and suffered the loss of two babies to miscarriage in between. "Pain in childbearing"[5] means a great many things to me now. But I did not expect to think or talk about birth as much as I did during the days my mom was dying. I certainly didn't expect giving birth to somehow *prepare* me for it.

But death, it turns out, is a lot like birth. There is a cadence to the way we leave this world that echoes the rhythm with which we arrive. I may not have noticed it had I not delivered my third child, Ruby, just five months before midwifing my mom through her final days. But I'm not the only one nodding to this reality.

"The beginning of life and the end are so similar," Francesca Arnoldy told *The New York Times*. "The intensity of it, the mystery, all of the unknowns. You have to relinquish your sense of control and agenda and ride it out, and be super attentive in the moment."[6]

Arnoldy is the lead instructor of a certificate program at the University of Vermont that trains end-of-life doulas—1,400 of them between 2017 and 2021. The doula title comes from the Greek word for female servant, *doulé*.[7] Like birth doulas, end-of-life doulas come alongside medical workers and family members

---

5. "To the woman [God] said, 'I will surely multiply your pain in childbearing; in pain you shall bring forth children'" (Gen. 3:16).

6. Abby Ellin, "'Death Doulas' Provide Aid at the End of Life," NYTimes.com, June 24, 2021, www.nytimes.com/2021/06/24/well/doulas-death-end-of-life.

7. According to Strong's Greek concordance, this is the word Mary uses for herself when the angel tells her she will be with child: "Behold, I am the servant of the Lord" (Luke 1:38, 48). It is also used in Acts 2:18 to refer to female servants of the Lord who will receive God's Spirit.

to help loved ones laboring toward death navigate their final days.

A friend of mine is a doula who assists with both births and deaths. She would tell you what I would: the stages of the birthing and the dying process mirror one another, like stair steps into and out of life. Though our sin is the cause of both birth pains[8] and death,[9] I have seen the fingerprints of God's kindness and design lingering on them both.

When I experienced labor, I was surprised to feel painless, blue-sky breaks between the gut-wrenching contractions. "What mercy!" I remember thinking, even as I braced myself for the next wave of pain. When my mom was laboring toward death, I felt God's compassion in that process too. I watched as bouts of restlessness and agitation gave way to stillness and acceptance, wave after wave of each bringing her closer to that final shore.

The early stages of both birth and death are often accompanied by feverish "nesting" behaviors, whether the person is preparing to welcome new loved ones to this world or to leave them behind in it. I scheduled grocery deliveries during the early hours of my last labor; my mom organized her upstairs office with the help of a friend in her final weeks, even though none of us could have numbered how few days she had left.

When the contractions pick up for a woman in labor, she loses interest in food and must be reminded to take sips of water. The dying one also forsakes the nourishment her loved ones still feel desperate to give her. Yes, both processes have aspects that

---

8. As a curse for sin, God said to Eve, "I will surely multiply your pain in childbearing; in pain you shall bring forth children" (Gen. 3:16).
9. "For the wages of sin is death" (Rom. 6:23).

feel counterintuitive. There is perhaps none more contrary than the need to stop feeding or hydrating a loved one whose body is in the process of shutting down.

And yet, I found it *benevolent* of God to take away the dying one's *desire* for food and water when the body can no longer process it. "Although we cringe at the thought of depriving loved ones of nourishment," Kathryn Butler, former ICU doctor and a believer, writes in *Between Life and Death*, some forms of forced nutrition during end stages can "actually worsen discomfort during our final days."[10]

Like midwives that expecting mothers call when they *think* they're in labor, hospice workers and others familiar with the dying process can make all the difference in discerning which stage a loved one is in—and how to comfort them in the midst of it. Hospice care not only aids those caring for the dying but can also greatly improve the quality and quantity of their final days.[11]

I value this sort of expertise so much that I hired a doula to help us through our first birth. And, when it was clear Mom was dying, in addition to having hospice workers in and out of the house her last week, we called a longtime friend who had worked as a hospice pastor to help us navigate the spiritual process unfolding alongside death. Though there are stages to both birth and death, there is no formula or predictable timetable to either. Both can be utterly disorienting.

---

10. Kathryn Butler, *Between Life and Death: A Gospel-Centered Guide to End-of-Life Medical Care* (Wheaton, IL: Crossway, 2019), 130.

11. Butler points out in her book that research indicates hospice improves survival. "In the final stages of chronic illness, *stopping aggressive treatment can prolong life.*"

As with birth, we have little control over when death arrives. There are medical interventions that permit us some semblance of influence over these comings and goings. Some, like scheduling a baby's delivery, are ethically neutral, guided by conscience and necessity. Others, like physician-assisted suicide, are what the Bible would consider a wrongful taking of the reins to end a life. But there are many gray areas in between.[12]

Both processes often come with a good deal of waiting, a waiting felt so bodily that it builds like a pent-up wave into yearning and longing. This is the sanctifying part. I read and reread the poem "Wait" by Russell Kelfer during the long days before Cora's birth:

> *You'd never know, should your pain quickly flee,*
> *What it means that My grace is sufficient for thee.*
> *Yes, your dearest dreams overnight would come true,*
> *But, oh, the loss, if you missed what I'm doing in you.*[13]

Birthing and dying are indeed formational processes. They leave us with new titles and transformed realities. And much of their good work is done in the waiting. Some long for years to become pregnant or to adopt a child as their own, wading through month after month of one-lined pregnancy tests or paperwork. Whether through adoption, foster care, or birth, the labor of

---

12. Consider the Butler book, *Between Life and Death*, in its entirety for a thorough treatment of the ethical considerations for Christians in making end-of-life medical decisions.
13. Russell Kelfer, "Wait," RussellKelfer.org, russellkelfer.org/poem-wait.htm. Used with permission.

providing for new life proves grueling and painstaking—even if it quickly gives way to joy.

Waiting for death is, of course, different. The deaths of loved ones, unlike their arrivals, are not something we intuitively want. But, once someone is afflicted with terminal illness, injury, or the frailty of age, there is a sense in which we begin to long for the end of their suffering. No mother longs for the pain of labor itself to come upon her—that is, not until she's been pregnant for a good long while. There does—trust me—come a day when the pain of delivery becomes more desirable than waddling full-bellied through another August afternoon.

And I wonder if these themes are evidence of a good design. Would we ever long for heaven if the world didn't disappoint us sometimes? "For we know that the whole creation has been groaning together in the pains of childbirth until now. And not only the creation, but we ourselves, who have the firstfruits of the Spirit, groan inwardly as we wait eagerly for adoption as sons, the redemption of our bodies" (Rom. 8:22–23).

This verse comes to life when we are waiting and longing for new birth—whether it arrives through the first squalls of a newborn or through the final breaths of a Christian aching for eternal life in Christ. In both processes, we groan as we wait. Our bodies bend and writhe with the waves of birth pains, and they grow still as the indescribable dawns.

I've come to think of birth and death not as natural phenomena that the Bible distantly observes and then uses to teach us. No. These bookends are carefully crafted components of our lives in a world and in bodies handmade by a God *who was born to die.*

"We see God's invisible attributes in the things he has made, and the only correct response is to worship him," Gloria Furman writes in her book *Labor with Hope*. "Jesus has written us into his story, and he designed birth to glorify himself."[14]

I believe He designed death—*even death*—to do that too.

BIRTHED AGAIN

In the wee hours of the morning after Thanksgiving, a day before Mom would leave us, I wandered from an upstairs guest room down to her bedside. I had been awake, feeding my five-month-old daughter, Ruby, when something came to my mind. I wanted to tell Mom while I still could.

As much as I had learned to laugh about my first "birth plan" and all my darling hopes for Cora's delivery, I now wished I had a plan like that for Mom's death. Now that she was no longer able to talk, did she want music playing in the background or just quiet? Did she want a rotating door of visitors or just family by her side?

When I was in the room, I instinctively played songs from the Spotify playlist I'd put together to get me through childbirth. It seems fitting to me now that lyrics from "We Will Feast in the House of Zion" and "Dear Refuge of My Weary Soul" carried us through Ruby's coming and Mom's going that year. They were similar in so many ways, arriving on terms entirely outside my control.

14. Gloria Furman, *Labor with Hope* (Wheaton, IL: Crossway, 2019), 92–93.

Ruby was delivered under duress, you might say, three weeks before her due date during the pandemic summer of 2020. My belly and the baby had stopped growing on pace, so I knew I would be monitored the day after we got back from a quick escape to the nearest beach.

To make matters worse, the ceiling in our bedroom had fallen in a couple weeks before—a symptom of poor construction and the constant rattle of helicopters overhead in Northern Virginia. All our baby clothes were still in the attic when I showed up to my appointment.

"God, I'm not ready," I prayed. "Please let the baby stay in there."

It's hard to tell how concerned a doctor is when you can only see the top half of her face over a mask. But I knew from the eyebrows of the one measuring the flow of blood from the placenta to the baby that when she said, "We need to deliver this baby," she meant it. Apparently, placentas can quit doing their job. Mine had shared space with a large blood clot at the beginning of the pregnancy, which had come on the heels of a miscarriage. This had not been an easy ride. Now, they told me, the placenta appeared to be decaying early. The baby, no longer getting enough nourishment, had stopped growing.

I went to my car to grab a poorly packed hospital bag. Plopping into the driver's seat for a moment, I let the tears come. "I'm not ready," I prayed again. "But am I ever?" As I sat there, palms up on my lap, one word washed again and again into my mind: "Receive."

Thirty-three hours later, and some fifteen hours after my induction, I was still having trouble doing just that. The midwife overseeing what had become my longest labor yet wheeled over on a stool to face me.

"How badly did you want to give birth today?" she asked.

"Zero percent," I said between contractions. A few hours ago, I was still planning what the other two kids would eat while friends from church watched them. I was still wishing I'd had another week or two to prepare. Now I was leaning against the bed rail, going through the motions of an unmedicated childbirth while really just wishing it were over.

"Right. And I think your body knows that," she said. "I think you are fighting yourself, and you need a little help to relax into this process."

This midwife knew my history, knew my propensity toward natural-as-possible births. But she also knew when to intervene.

In a flash, I remembered the eyebrows of concern stitched across the doctor's face who had monitored the baby. I thought of the friends with whom we'd recently grieved the birth of a precious stillborn child. I thought of all that was at stake—and of the joy set before me, a baby just a few pushes away.

"Receive," I thought. And I relented.

After sixteen hours of labor—and an hour after an epidural forced me to receive this birth on terms that were not quite my own—our dear tiny Ruby was born.

This is the story I told Mom that Thanksgiving night, even though she already knew every detail of it, even though she had paced the floors a few states away as it unfolded.

Now, I leaned over the still frame of a woman who had never

stopped moving and whispered, "Mama, I know it feels like so much is still unfinished." I watched her eyebrows—the only part of her that still moved—crease with emotion. I knew she could hear.

"I can't tell you that we won't keep needing you once you're not here," I sniffled. "But you know as well as I do that your eternal rest does not depend on whether you finished all the work you set out to do. It depends on whether Christ did."

Christ's labor of love on the cross was not ineffectual. It did not stall out. It achieved through great groaning exactly what He set out for it to achieve, for the joy set before Him.[15] And Christ's death and resurrection didn't just birth new life in us. They put an end to the birth pains of death.

"The cords of death" that David felt wrapping around his neck in Psalm 18 can also be translated as *the birth pains of death*."[16] Jesus felt these too and prayed in the midst, "Now is my soul troubled. And what shall I say? 'Father, save me from this hour'? But for this purpose I have come to this hour" (John 12:27).

Our Savior felt the particular pains we feel when death approaches. But He also cut them short.[17] The cords of death that nearly strangled David no longer have a chokehold on us. Christ's resurrection—and the seed of our own—have put an end to death's reign of fear.[18]

---

15. Hebrews 12:2.

16. Gloria Furman writes in *Labor with Hope* that the Greek translation of "the cords of death encompassed me" in Psalm 18:4 is literally "*the birth pains of death* encompassed me."

17. When God raised Christ from the dead, He loosed, or put an end to, "the pangs of death" (Acts 2:24).

18. Christ "too shared in their humanity so that by his death he might break the power of him who holds the power of death—that is, the devil—and free those who all their lives were held in slavery by their fear of death" (Heb. 2:14–15 NIV).

Birth and death are still painful, transformational experiences. But, for those who trust in Christ, even death becomes a delivery room.[19]

---

19. "Whoever believes in me, though he die, yet shall he live" (John 11:25b).

SEVEN

Letting Go, Coming Alive

Christ leads me through no darker rooms
Than he went through before;
And he that in God's Kingdom comes
Must enter by this door.[1]

—RICHARD BAXTER (1615–1691)

"The Lord goes before you," I repeated to myself as I steered our white minivan on a now-familiar route to the nearest children's hospital. I breathed in the late-setting August sun beyond my rearview mirror and prayed again anyway, "Go before us, Lord; make a way."

For the third time in a week, one of us was headed to an emergency room with our five-year-old, Cora. On and off for the past week, we'd found her hunched over in bed or pacing the floor,

---

1. Richard Baxter, "Christ Leads Me Through No Darker Rooms" (1615–1691), Hymnary. org. Language updated for clarity.

writhing with stomach pain and vomiting. ER doctors had sent us home twice with a run-of-the-mill constipation diagnosis. But I knew in my gut something else was wrong.

By 1 a.m. the night of our third visit, a pediatric radiologist was pressing an ultrasound wand under Cora's ribs and showing me what it was on the black-and-white screen, something "that shouldn't be there," he said.[2]

"That's her pancreas," he said, pointing to a blur of organs, "and that's her bowel . . . but I don't know what that is."

Over the course of that week, we'd come to call the "fluid-filled structure" a cyst. But, at nearly 7 centimeters long and 5 centimeters across, it was larger than the little word implied, measuring about the same size as her little-girl stomach. Her symptoms indicated it had grown over time and was now putting pressure on her digestive system. It needed to come out.

The day after we got home from that first hospital stay, I was sitting on the back porch making calls, kids playing nearby and ten-week-old Ruby in my lap. I needed to get Cora scheduled for another scan and then for major abdominal surgery. I had called and prayed and pushed and called again. The earliest anyone could get us in was weeks away. Discouraged, I broke down and called the woman who by now had practically earned a PhD in medical frustrations: my mom.

"How do I know when to keep advocating and when to let it go?" I asked her, tears brimming over. "They can't get her in for

---

2. Another physician later told us that emergency room doctors are trained to find "horses"—shorthand for routine illnesses—"not zebras." Finding that rare cyst was like finding a zebra. In other words, a miracle.

weeks, Mom! Why can't they get her in?"

"Oh, honey," she said, her softness surprising me. "You've done enough for today."

I had fully expected her to start picking up the phone herself, to make things happen, as she always did. Instead, she said, "Just let it be for now."

The next day, a scheduler with whom I'd left a message called back and said there had been a cancellation. She could get us in for the scan that week. "It's by divine intervention that you called," she said. *Amen*, I thought, *and probably the prayers of at least two mothers.*

Less than three weeks later, the day after Cora's sixth birthday, I journaled a prayer the morning of what would be a seven-hour wait, followed by a five-hour surgery. I told the Lord that handing over my little girl to this surgeon felt like Abraham walking Isaac up the hill. I would not be lifting the knife, but someone would, even if it was for her ultimate good.

The writer of Hebrews tells us "Abraham reasoned that if Isaac died, God was able to bring him back to life again. And in a sense, Abraham did receive his son back from the dead" (Heb. 11:19 NLT).

Could I believe that too?

In the end, Cora came through the surgery just fine, an Ebenezer of God's faithfulness stitched across her abdomen. I stood back and watched as the young seed of faith God had planted in her blossomed under trial, as she knelt to pray on her own before an X-ray and laughed her way through days without food. I realized that God could call my daughter into—and use mightily—difficult trials I never would have chosen.

But I didn't know then just how soon my mom would have to take the letting-go advice she had just given me.

The day after pathologists confirmed that Cora's cyst was not cancerous, allowing us to tie a tiny bow on the trial those weeks had been, we turned to face a new one. We were sitting down to Friday-night pizza when I got a text from Mom. A routine scan showed fluid was building up in her abdomen. She was headed to the ER to see if they could drain it.

I felt a burning sensation in my own stomach as I Googled the symptom, finding a name for it. Ascites, the internet told me, "is a manifestation of end stage events in a variety of cancers . . . associated with significant morbidity."[3] *This*, it slowly dawned on me, *is what it looks like to die of cancer.* This was the beginning of the end.

For the first time, I knew that what she was experiencing was not from the cocktail of medicines she'd been on for years, but from the cancer itself. The organs to which the cancer had spread, including her lungs and liver, were increasingly unable to do their jobs, causing unfiltered fluid to build up over time. Mom, who often preferred to put a positive spin on whatever her doctors were telling her, could not sugar-coat this one.

Neither of us said it out loud, but we both knew what this meant. As much as she didn't want to let go of the world that contains us, she would have to soon.

---

3. (Ascites is pronounced *uh-SAI-teez*.) Dr. A. A. Ayantunde, "Pattern and Prognostic Factors in Patients with Malignant Ascites: A Retrospective Study," Annals of Oncology, May 01, 2007, https://www.annalsofoncology.org/article/S0923-7534(19)42020-6/fulltext.

LOOSENING THE GRIP

Sometimes, we have a sense of what's coming. Mary, the mother of Jesus, did. And she "treasured up" all the things that had been told her about this son of hers who was really the Son of God (Luke 2:19, 51). The Greek word used for treasuring means "to preserve a thing from perishing or being lost" or to "keep in mind . . . lest it be forgotten."[4] I don't think Mary was at risk of forgetting what she was being told, but she marveled at it all the same.

Mary's meditating is a thread running across the second chapter of Luke's gospel, inviting us to look *through the mother's eyes* at the Savior's unexpected life and predicted death.

When shepherds sprint to the manger where she's just given birth, breathless from their run-in with a heavenly host of messengers, Mary ponders what they tell her: *This baby in your arms is the Savior of us all, Christ the Lord.* Mary marvels again when an old prophet confirms this, and adds: *This salvation will come through a sword that will also pierce your own soul.* And when the child, now a boy, reminds His parents to remember that He belongs, first and foremost, to the Father, Mary treasures it all up again.[5]

From day one, the young mother Mary was learning to let go of the One she had welcomed into this world. She meditated on who He was becoming, and what it would require of her. She was doing in a very literal way what every mother must do. One day, we watch ours drive away in a car. One day, she watched hers die on a cross.

---

4. "Lexicon: Strong's G4933 *syntēreō*," Blue Letter Bible, https://www.blueletterbible.org/lexicon/g4933/esv/mgnt/0-1/.
5. These stories are summaries of Luke 2, specifically verses 8–19; 22–35; and 41–50.

But Mary's letting go became the way for all of us to receive. Her arms were left empty, yet "from [Christ's] fullness we have all received, grace upon grace" (John 1:16).

Letting go is never as easy as Elsa in the Disney movie *Frozen* makes it sound.[6] It certainly wasn't for my mom. Divorce, in particular, has a way of interrupting the slow process of raising children to one day release them into the world. Custody battles have a way of tightening the grip at stages when it should instead begin to loosen.

Once Mom was diagnosed with cancer, her fears of "losing us" morphed into fears of losing her own life—and us in the process. Her attachments toward my sister and me grew even stronger. As I married, moved away, and had my own children, I found the cords that still bound us together a little stifling at times.[7]

Exhibit A was the way she hugged me. If Mom was about to leave our home in Virginia or we had just arrived at hers for a holiday, her embrace could last for entire minutes. She would squeeze, then sigh, then squeeze again, like a boa constrictor getting warmed up. I was a daughter who had years ago spread her wings and now felt them literally pinned to my sides.

Often, my own arms would hang limp in resignation, refusing

---

6. Idina Menzel, "Let It Go!" *Frozen*, Walt Disney Records, 2013.

7. It can feel odd to tell stories about our loved ones who are no longer here. Should we relay only the good and forget the difficult parts? I've wrestled with that in these pages. In the end, I've tried to strike a balance between being both honest about and honoring toward those I've loved. I hope it grants you permission to do the same. There are aspects of our relationships that we get to come to terms with, even grieve, long after the other person is gone. Ignoring those parts doesn't make them go away. In this chapter, I hope to show that God was at work in my mom to the very end, shaping her more and more into His image. She was a whole, beautiful, needy human-in-progress—and so am I.

to participate in what these hugs had to say but knowing I couldn't pull away. "I'm dying, you know," her squeeze spoke over me. "Not today, but sometime soon. And I'm going to hug you like it."

No, letting go was not easy for Mom. She knew it too. In 2014, the year my first daughter was born, Mom wrote in her journal: "Why do I struggle so in giving up and letting go?" An English major, Mom answered her own question with a Shakespearean lilt: "Fear that the journey to which my foot is set will be too hard to bear?"

One way or another, we all let go of what used to be. Sometimes we see the need to release something or someone and do so voluntarily, however hard it may still be. Other times, the past is ripped from our hands, leaving us raw and reeling. Often, though, these transitions look a lot more like making it across monkey bars at a playground. We let go of what was, only to reach for what is coming.

This is the essence of growing up, for both the parent and the child. We leave behind burp cloths and reach for Band-Aids. We surrender soccer shin guards for SAT-prep tests. Drivers' licenses, sure enough, mean that one day the child will drive away. We don't long for the letting go, but we know somehow that the process of moving toward it one rung at a time has prepared us for it.

A similar reality plays out at the end of life. For the Christian, death is not just letting go of the life we've known. It is also a reaching for the new life we've been promised in Christ.

As Paul told the Philippians, "For to me to live is Christ, and *to die is gain*." Paul said he was "hard pressed" to decide between the two. His "desire is to depart and be with Christ, for that is far better" (Phil. 1:21, 23).

Peter calls this far better thing our "living hope," and it is earned and proven to us "through the resurrection of Jesus Christ from the dead." This is the hope that comes to life when this life falls short and fails. This is the hope that comes to life in the face of death. Unlike our bodies, it cannot be taken from us. This eternal inheritance, Peter tells us in abundant language, is "imperishable, undefiled, and unfading, kept in heaven for you" (1 Peter 1:3–4).

When we let go of this life, this is the hope we're reaching for. And when we watch someone who trusts in this hope die, we also get to see them come to life.

COMING ALIVE

"Mom, can I be honest?" I ask over the phone, walking a slow loop around the cul-de-sac outside our house. It's October and the vermillion-leaved tree that leans a little too far over the walkway is glowing under an early evening sun. I sense in my bones that the autumn of Mom's life is also underway.

"Yes," she says, her voice so scratchy I can feel the dryness in my own throat. It has gotten so much worse in the two weeks since she visited us here—too sick to have traveled, but doing it anyway—and in the three weeks since the fluid buildup began.

"Because I don't necessarily feel how you feel right now. I know this is your process, and I don't want to get in the way of that," I venture, remembering a conversation we'd had in my living room and how upset she got when I implied this might be the end.

But she interrupts, "It's your process too."

She hears me sniffling rather than continuing, so she says it again, soothing, "It's okay. It's okay."

I can hear her ache to comfort me, and I feel it. It resonates in a new way, having so recently wished to take the pain of surgery from my own daughter, to pull the hurt out of her frame and absorb it somehow into my own.

"I know you need to focus on the positive to keep going, to keep fighting," I start, "but is it okay if I just don't feel positive?"

"Yes," her calm tone is assuring, but I don't trust it fully.

"Because I feel like I'm going to show up at Thanksgiving and everyone's gonna want to *enjoy the holiday* and be happy and— what if I can't? What if I'm just really sad? Because, Mom . . . I'm really, really sad."

I dare to continue, and it spills out: "I know that nobody wants to talk about it—that I'm not supposed to talk about it— but, I feel like you're dying." I rush ahead before the courage runs out, "And I can't be happy when I feel that way. I'm just so sad."

The tears take over, cooling the heat of my emotions as they run down my cheeks and soak into the collar of my sweater. I sniffle louder than I'd like and scan the horizon for neighbors.

"Oh, honey," she says, her voice full of emotion. "It's okay."

Wait, I think, *she's not going to correct me? Tell me she's not dying? That she'll be fine? That I've got it all wrong?*

"This is hard," she says.

"That's okay," she says.

"You can feel how you need to feel, and that's okay."

I ended the phone call, thunderstruck. Had my mom really just let this be *about me*?

At the moment when she was bearing the full weight of her sickness, her fading, her feelings, she was making space for mine. Given our history, the way her narrative of events seemed to often eclipse my own, I could hardly believe it. Suddenly, rather than forcing me to feel what she was feeling—like she had with all those long hugs over the years—she was letting me feel and express something different.

Her words on that call held me in an entirely different way. I felt the overwhelming warmth of being let go, yet held, of being loved. And I knew it was the sacrificial kind.

This was the second time in as many months that I noticed her laying down her desires for mine in areas that had been hard in the past. There was a particular weekend in October that Mom wanted to visit, but I told her that it would not work well for us. Usually, this didn't stop her from coming anyway, especially if she had a pressing medical appointment and wanted to get a dose of courage from seeing her grandkids beforehand. But, when that excuse was truer than ever, she did not use it.

When I said the weekend didn't work, she simply said, "That's fine. Is there another one that would?" I pulled the phone away from my ear to confirm I was talking to my mother. Was this really her? When she knew we didn't have much time left together, was she really letting it be on my terms? Her words, so simply spoken, were a balm for old wounds, one that continued healing even after she was gone. They were evidence that, as she was dying to this world and all its hopes and futures, she was coming alive to the next, to the reality that could not be taken from her.

Later, with the help of our friend Susan Arner, a former hospice pastor, I was able to name what I'd witnessed on that call and in a handful of other experiences during Mom's final weeks.[8] As Mom stopped clinging to physical healing in this life—and to us—she was able to reach for a different sort of healing in the next. As her body began to fade, the Spirit in her was coming more and more alive.

FLASHES OF LIFE

As Christians, we may have sixty years left to live or far fewer. But Romans 6 tells us we are each, instantly, at conversion "united" with Christ "in a death like his." This means we can also "certainly be united with him in a resurrection like his" (v. 5). This is the truth we rehearse and embody when we go through the waters of baptism.

Our church, like many, started conducting baptisms outside during the pandemic. What started as a way to return to the basics of worship while still holding outdoor services turned into a beloved tradition that allowed more of us to gather in one space. So, for one-service Sundays a few times a year, we still break out the outdoor baptismal—an aluminum horse trough just long enough to fit the tallest of adults.

What the makeshift font lacks in formality it makes up for in proximity. From our folding chairs strewn under shade tents

---

8. Susan had been on our church's staff leading my sister's middle school youth group, years before, and we had long ago adopted her into our family. It is sheer mercy that she had served a stint as a hospice pastor in the intervening years and would later arrive in time to walk with us through Mom's final hours.

about the grass, the congregation can see in up-close detail the reality being reenacted at eye level.

"Buried in the likeness of Christ's death," the pastor proclaims as he lowers a woman into the water one sunlit Sunday, her adult son looking on. "Raised in the likeness of His resurrection!"

The woman comes up smiling, a jet-black ponytail sopping at her neck, and we bear witness with our happy tears, shaken loose by applause. Her testimony tells us she has lived long enough and lost enough to know that the life she died to pales in comparison to the one she's receiving. We can see it in her every fiber.

"Those who place their faith in Christ," theologian F. F. Bruce writes, "are united with him by that faith—united so closely that his experience now becomes theirs: they share his death to the old order ('under law') . . . and his resurrection to new life."[9]

The Christ follower dies to self and to sin. They die to this world through suffering. They die by degrees as their flesh fades. And, in all their dying, they are comforted by the knowing companionship of Christ.

The apostle Paul saw this as a given: "Do you not know that all of us who have been baptized into Christ Jesus were baptized into his death? We were buried therefore with him by baptism into death, in order that, just as Christ was raised from the dead by the glory of the Father, we too might walk in newness of life" (Rom. 6:3–4).

This newness of life begins at salvation, yes. But it doesn't end there. It continues to dawn across our lives through the ongoing work of sanctification, through the painstaking putting off of the

9. F. F. Bruce, *The Epistle to the Galatians: A Commentary on the Greek Text, New International Greek Testament Commentary* (Grand Rapids, MI: W. B. Eerdmans Pub. Co., 1982), 144.

old self and the putting on of the new. But the moment when this newness of life reaches its fullness is not when we pass through the brief waters of baptism. It is when we walk through the unknowable waters of our own death.

At this precipice, everything that used to matter too much in this life no longer does. Everything that will matter for eternity crystallizes into urgent focus. Will the unseen planks of faith—the only hope for being carried across death's great abyss—really hold? In this moment of great testing, we need only *see our need* for the way across to do what the thief hanging next to Christ did—to look to Jesus and live.[10]

It is then that our coming alive comes true—fully, irreversibly, miraculously.

As Christians, we're all told to "consider [ourselves] dead to sin and alive to God in Christ Jesus" (Rom. 6:11). But this truth has a way of coming to life when we watch believers, stripped of all else, clothe themselves in it near the end of life. As the body that has known only this world fades, the God-in-them seems to dawn more fully on the horizon, spreading warmth to broken places we thought were beyond repair.

I think of this as I see the children of our church watching wide-eyed while others are baptized. I wonder if the idea of speaking up front or of being submerged, if only for a moment, is scary to them. After the service, though, I watch a handful of them make their way to the water trough. They stick their hands in the cool water, first out of curiosity, then for refreshment.

10. Luke 23:39–43.

Eventually, they start to splash and play in these waters we use to rehearse salvation.

I wonder if I should stop this group of kids that includes my son, now soaked to the bone. But I also wonder if their repeated exposure, if their sheer proximity to these waters, will make it easier to enter themselves one day.

I believe it does for death. Walking alongside others through their final days is a privilege—and a tender dress rehearsal for our own.

The hidden beauty of knowing a loved one is dying is this: tucked into the folds of their fading are flashes of the new life that's beginning. Yes, there is fear, even doubt; a night of the soul that gets darker before the dawn. Christ acknowledged both the darkness and the trust in the midst of His own death: "My God, my God, why have you forsaken me?" He said (Matt. 27:46), before saying, "Father, into your hands I commit my spirit!" (Luke 23:46).

There are whispers of the dawn's eternal healing in the life of a Christ-follower too even before it arrives: in the mother who writes a letter to say she's sorry, in the son's last voicemail before the hike that took his life, in the grandmother's receiving of the help she always said she didn't want. There is a letting go of this world and a reaching for the next, a preview of the renewal to come.

In Christ, there will come a time when we no longer have to "put to death" what is earthly in us, when death puts it to death for us.[11] There will come a time when it no longer requires great

---

11. "Put to death therefore what is earthly in you: sexual immorality, impurity, passion, evil desire, and covetousness, which is idolatry" (Col. 3:5).

effort to set our minds on things above as we enter the very gates that hold them.[12] What we've seen in a mirror dimly will take full, glorious shape.

If Christ has been "put to death in the flesh but made alive in the spirit" (1 Peter 3:18b), so then are we. The pattern holds. It holds those we love, and it can hold each of us too.

12. "If then you have been raised with Christ, seek the things that are above, where Christ is, seated at the right hand of God" (Col. 3:1).

EIGHT

Coming Home, Caregiving

Love is wearying in this way,
and even we who deeply love the ones we serve,
need grace upon grace upon grace.[1]

—DOUGLAS KAINE MCKELVEY, *EVERY MOMENT HOLY, VOLUME II*

I had nearly forgotten the otherworldly glow of a Kansas sunset, the way a pale-blue sky bleeds into raucous pinks and oranges at the horizon line, picking up color like kernels of wheat from the amber waves of grain. But there it was, welcoming me back with a beauty so familiar it stirred longing from a deep well within.

At the edge of my vision, a white-breasted kestrel hunting the ditches caught my eye, and Rich Mullins's words about a hawk

---

1. Douglas Kaine McKelvey, "A Liturgy for Those Who Tend a Loved One in Decline," *Every Moment Holy, Volume II* (Nashville: Rabbit Room Press, 2021), 17.

bursting into flight at sunset—the soundtrack of these plains—filled my mind.[2]

And I prayed along with the rest of the song to the God whose name I too have heard these prairies praise,[3] to the God who alone knew what we were driving toward that day.

Something widens inside me when I leave the tree-canopied streets of Virginia and reenter the open-sky country of Kansas, if only for a holiday visit. It's like letting out a breath I didn't know I'd been holding. "There you are," I say to a part of myself that's still rooted to these grasslands, to the rare and tender feeling of being both known and loved.

I felt the lightness of a homecoming that late-November evening—alongside a heaviness I could not shake.

"I'm coming home to begin walking Mom home," I typed into my phone notes from the passenger seat, the sun sinking into the Flint Hills before us. "I can't imagine her not being here. But I know soon she won't be."

I didn't know *how* soon. My sister and I were pretty sure before we arrived that this would be Mom's last holiday season. None of us expected she would barely make it through Thanksgiving that week.

I got my first clue when we pulled into the driveway. For the

---

2. "Calling Out Your Name" by Rich Mullins, © 1990 BMG Songs, Inc. (ASCAP), *The World as Best as I Remember It, Volume One* (Nashville: Reunion, 1991).

3. According to the book *An Arrow Pointing to Heaven*, a devotional biography about Rich Mullins by James Bryan Smith, Mullins finished writing this song after a motorcycle ride through Kansas's Flint Hills. "He saw that we live in a God-bathed universe," writes Smith, who hosted Mullins during his time in my hometown of Wichita, Kan. "For Rich, there was too much beauty around him for two eyes to see, but he did his best, and he wrote songs that help the rest of us catch a glimpse of what he saw." (Nashville: B & H, 2000), 103.

first time I could recall, Mom wasn't waving at me from the front stoop, barely waiting for the car to stop before unbuckling a grandchild or circling in for an exuberant hug. I opened the front door of the house to find she couldn't even rise to greet us, a walker perched nearby testifying to her rapid decline.

Fully reclined in a living room chair and flanked by beverages and medications, Mom looked like the ultrasoft fabric of her favorite robe and blanket might swallow her whole. A shell of the woman I knew, her brown eyes were now floating in deeper, darker sockets and her cheeks and collarbones were jutting out. She had shed at least twenty-five pounds and the last wisps of her white hair in the six weeks since I'd seen her, a more intense chemotherapy and the spreading cancer taking their cumulative toll.

As she hugged our oldest daughter, who got to her first, I saw a desperate hunger in Mom's embrace, a *finally-you're-here* look that was markedly new. And something broke inside me. "This is it," my gut whispered, though my head wasn't ready to receive it. When people say, "My heart went out to her," this is the feeling they're trying to describe. Her body, breaking down right before me, moved my own into action.

In an instant, the deeply-rooted roles of mother and child were reversed. My sister would experience something similar when she got to town the next day. We were here to care for *her*.

CAREGIVING

We begin and end our lives in weakness. Each of us will one day be as dependent on others in our dying days as we were on our mothers at birth. If we love and are loved by others, we are likely to find ourselves in caregiving roles for which there may not be nine months to prepare.

One in five Americans is currently providing unpaid care for an adult who needs medical or functional help, according to the AARP's most recent survey of caregiving.[4] And a quarter of them are caring for more than one person at the same time. These numbers will continue to rise as America's fertility rate declines and its overall population ages. By 2030, demographers predict that the number of people sixty-five and older in the United States will for the first time eclipse the number of children.

The need is great. The work is hard. But sometimes we need to be reminded that it's also *good*, in the fullest sense of the word.

It is weighty to be needed in this way. There is a feeling, in the very thick of it, that there is nowhere else in the world your body should be, no greater work for it to do, than to be caring for this person. Then, a moment later, the gravity of the work feels crushing. You think—and then feel guilty for thinking—"How much longer can I do this?"

The average length of time spent in elder caregiving is four years.[5] *Four years* of filling out doctor's office forms and worrying about falls in the middle of the night. Four years of counting out pills and delivering meals. Fifteen percent of caregivers spend

---

4. The Caregiving in the US Survey is conducted every five years by the AARP, and the most recent one took place in 2020. "Caregiving in the United States, 2020," AARP.org, May 14, 2020, https://www.aarp.org/ppi/info-2020/caregiving-in-the-united-states.html.

5. Family Caregiver Alliance, "Caregiver Statistics: Demographics," 2016, https://www.caregiver.org/resource/caregiver-statistics-demographics/.

more than a decade providing care for an aging parent.[6] When dementia is involved, that time period can be even more prolonged.

These statistics bear witness to the hard, unrelenting work of walking with others through the end of their days. This is a work that is beyond the capacity of many to do on their own, especially when they are still working or caring for children. If you feel guilty for not "being there" for a loved one in the way you wanted to— or for not really wanting to—you're not alone. This unrelenting work often comes at the cost of many other good things. Yes, we can serve others out of the grace God supplies. But when we fail to or fall short of expectations—whether ours or those of others— we can also receive grace. No loved one of yours has suffered beyond the sight of the One who feeds every bird and adorns every flower.[7] His arm is not shortened by our shortcomings. Rather, He gives grace upon grace.[8]

I have often felt like I fell short of the high caregiving bar set by my own mother. Mom cared for her mom over a much longer period of decline until Grandma died in 2018. I know how it pained and consumed Mom to watch her mother slowly lose her

---

6. CareChoice, "An Intuitive Guide to Harmony for Those Who Feel Trapped Caring for Their Elderly Parent," GetCareChoice.com, 2021, https://getcarechoice.com/post/trapped-caring-for-elderly-parent/#:~:text=The%20average%20length%20of%20time,day%20on%20their%20caregiving%20responsibilities. (Note: I do not condone the tenor of this article, which implies that elderly parents are such a burden that paid care is a given. But I do think it exemplifies modern attitudes on this front and reveals the need for nuance while discerning caregiving options.)

7. "Look at the birds of the air: they neither sow nor reap nor gather into barns, and yet your heavenly Father feeds them. Are you not of more value than they?" (Matt. 6:26). See also verses 25–33.

8. "For from his fullness we have all received, grace upon grace" (John 1:16).

independence over a long stretch of years. I saw how thoroughly she cared for her, even when her own body began to fail. She couldn't have done it, though, without the help of Grandma's devoted companion, Steve LeDou, who made it possible for her to continue living at home.

For the Christian, the command to care well for those who need it, and for aging relatives in particular, is explicit. In his letters to Timothy, Paul spills much ink ensuring the widows and needy are cared for—first by their own families, and then by the church:

> Honor widows who are truly widows. But if a widow has children or grandchildren, let them first learn to show godliness to their own household and to make some return to their parents, *for this is pleasing in the sight of God*... But if anyone does not provide for his relatives, and especially for members of his household, he has denied the faith and is worse than an unbeliever." (1 Tim. 5:3–4, 8)

There is an expectation here that children and grandchildren care for the relatives who cared for them. But Paul makes it clear that this is more than an obligation: caring for the elderly in a family and in the family of God is a work that is *pleasing* in the sight of God.

James adds that visiting widows in their affliction is a primary marker of true belief, an action that conveys trust in and reliance on the generous care of God (James 1:27). Why do we need to be reminded of this, both in biblical times and now? Because caring for those who are aging and needy does not feel remotely productive. In some cases, it can be downright unpleasant.

It does not feel nearly as valuable as it is. It does not feel as important as the also-grueling work of raising up a child who will contribute to society and, one hopes, care for the parent someday. It is an act, in the best of circumstances, done not in hope of return but in gratitude for what has already been.

And yet much caregiving is carried out *in spite of* the pain a loved one has caused or continues to inflict: A daughter battles bitterness and regret to faithfully care for a mother who wounded her deeply. A son wisely hires the right help when he needs a break from the hurtful comments that accompany his father's dementia. A husband endures to the end with a wife whose chronic deception and substance abuse shortened her life.

Each of these long-suffering servants adorns the doctrine of God our Savior, as Titus 2:10 says, often at great cost. If you're one of them, He sees you. He knows what it feels like to have someone spit in your face and to serve anyway. This, all of this, is the faithful stewarding of a human made in the image of God. It is often messy, always worthy work.

Boots-on-the-ground caregiving is also one of the ways God draws near to provide for His children in times of need. I've heard believers in the deepest trials describe it like this: it's harder to believe God is distant when His people keep showing up. In this way, they embody His promised care.

"When the righteous cry for help, the LORD hears and delivers them out of all their troubles. The LORD is near to the brokenhearted and saves the crushed in spirit. *Many are the afflictions of the righteous,* but the LORD delivers him out of them all" (Ps. 34:17–19).

Do you hear the promises tucked within? The Lord hears our cries from the pit of helplessness. And the Lord draws near to deliver. Yes, Christians participate in caregiving because it is a command and a calling for entire seasons of our lives. But we also draw near to the afflicted among us because *that is where God is.*

Marissa Bondurant, who wrote a Bible study for caregivers after shepherding her four-year-old daughter through cancer treatment,[9] later wrote on her blog about the particular privilege of being at her grandpa's bedside during his final days. "It was a difficult and yet beautiful moment in time where we rallied together to sacrificially serve one of our own," she said.[10] But the gift of that presence was not just for her grandpa; it was also for her. Looking back, Bondurant realized that "by a dying man's bedside is exactly where Jesus would be sitting . . . indeed *was* sitting."

THE CARE OF CHRIST

"Lord, he whom you love is ill."[11]

This is the message Martha and Mary sent to Jesus about their brother Lazarus. And with these words, John begins an elaborate retelling of Jesus' intimate, if at first confusing, form of caregiving for these three siblings.

The passage tells us that "Jesus loved Martha and her sister and

---

9. Marissa Bondurant, *Who Cares for You?: A 4-Week Bible Study for Caregivers* (Marissa Bondurant, 2023).

10. Marissa Bondurant, "If It's Not Okay, Then This is Not the End," Marissa Bondurant, November 16, 2022, https://marissabondurant.com/if-its-not-okay-then-this-is-not-the-end/.

11. John 11:3. For the full story, read John 11:1–53.

Lazarus," which makes what follows a little disconcerting: "So, when he heard that Lazarus was ill, he *stayed two days longer* in the place where he was" (John 11:5–6).

The One, whom the sisters knew had the power to heal their beloved brother when he was on his deathbed, did not run to his side. At their time of greatest need, He did not come right away. He tarried at a distance.

This is why, when Jesus finally came two days later, Martha said to Him, "Lord, *if you had been here,* my brother would not have died" (v. 21).

Do you hear the ache in her *if*?

"If you've been a Christian for a while, my guess is you can think of times when you've cried to God for help and felt like you got nothing back," Rebecca McLaughlin writes about this passage in her book, *Jesus Through the Eyes of Women*. "You've prayed for healing and it hasn't come. You've sent for Jesus and felt quite alone."[12]

This is often the experience of those who love or care for the desperately ill. At some point, the prayers for healing feel like they are bouncing off the ceiling. The God who says, "I will have compassion"[13] seems to have forgotten His pledge.

But when Jesus does arrive on the scene, we see more of what He's up to. We catch a glimpse into what He still does in this liminal space between our asking and His answer.

---

12. Rebecca McLaughlin, *Jesus Through the Eyes of Women: How the First Female Disciples Help Us Know and Love the Lord* (Austin, TX: The Gospel Coalition, 2022), 69.

13. Isaiah 54:7–8 speaks directly to experiences like this, yet from God's perspective. "'For a brief moment I deserted you, but with great compassion I will gather you. In overflowing anger for a moment I hid my face from you, but with everlasting love I will have compassion on you,' says the LORD, your Redeemer."

Jesus responds to Martha's lament not by telling her why He waited but by revealing who it is that stands before her: "I am the resurrection and the life," He says. "Whoever believes in me, though he die, yet shall he live, and everyone who lives and believes in me shall never die. Do you believe this?" (vv. 25–26).

In her deep pain and need, in the midst of feeling that the Lord didn't come through for her, Jesus tells Martha that what she really needs in this valley of the shadow of death is the One who is with her at that very moment—He who is *able* to resurrect both Lazarus and Martha from the dead, whether He does it right now or "on the last day" (v. 24b). What she needs, more than a resurrection, is the source of it.

After Martha calls for her, Mary repeats the same lament as her sister: "Lord, *if you had been here,* my brother would not have died" (vv. 28b, 32). Upon this second hearing of the sisters' aching *if,* Jesus does something extraordinary. The text tells us He was "deeply moved" and "greatly troubled" by the sight of their weeping, so much so that—when they direct Him to come and see the tomb—again, He does not go right away.

Instead, "Jesus wept" (v. 35).

The One who has the power to resurrect the dead—who would soon prove that power by raising four-day-dead Lazarus from the grave—paused to weep.

The God who *seems* far off when we cry out on behalf of a loved one is, in fact, drawing near in our time of need. He comes close to reveal Himself as the One we need more than answers, more than earthly healing, as the One who *enters into* our suffering. Even when He does not stop the pain right away, we can be reminded that, one day, He will. And we can know, right now, that He weeps with us.[14]

"When, at long last, Jesus comes to Mary, he sheds tears with her," McLaughlin explains. "He hadn't stayed away because he didn't care. He stayed away because he *did* care. The best thing he could give these siblings, whom he profoundly loved, was not immediate answer to their prayers, but revelation of himself."[15]

Jesus would go on to do more than the sisters imagined that day. He would not stop their brother's death; He would undo it. He said, "Lazarus, come out," and the dead man did. In an act that would seal His own death warrant, Jesus raised His beloved friend from the grave.

"I am the resurrection and the life," Jesus told Martha. "Do you believe this?"

Those of us who are caring for the sick and dying live in the moment that follows that question for now. We have begged God to heal, and we are reckoning with the fact that He may not. But we are also looking forward to the resurrection. In the midst of our waiting, this story reminds us that Jesus is not as far off as He might feel. His nearness, His weeping with us, is the fuel that helps us keep going in the hard work of comforting, caregiving, and grieving.

14. Bethany Barnard's song "Tears On Your Face" (All My Questions, 2021) is a beautiful meditation on this passage and on a Savior who doesn't see our pain from far away but draws near to grieve with us.

15. McLaughlin, *Jesus Through the Eyes of Women*, 69.

CARING FOR MOM

In the weeks between Mom's last visit to us and our visit to Kansas, every meal I made was, in my mind, for her. I would slice the sourdough and imagine her putting far too much blackberry jam on it, telling me a story about her dad's loaves. I would stir the sauce for enchiladas and realize I hadn't made them for her yet. Something deep inside me longed to nourish her, or to at least be close enough that I could.

But, once I got to town, it became clear that nourishment was no longer what she needed. Still-full cups of protein shakes languished on her side table as thrush, a yeast infection common with end-of-life cancer, blanketed her mouth and throat with sores. Swallowing anything, even the pain pills, made her wince as though gulping down shards of glass. No, food would no longer be a comfort.

"Mom," I asked one afternoon, instead of offering yet another drink, "would you like to take a shower?"

She nodded.

My mom had spent much of that year designing and oversee-ing renovations to the master bathroom, her latest in a series of home projects she could manage increasingly from bed. The project had recently passed the finish line, and I was as keen as she was to spend extra time in this space that bore her creative fingerprints.

With quick, searching steps, she somehow made it across the house from the living room. The pace could not conceal, though, the hunching of her upper body, the way she clung to the rolling walker and withered winded into the high-backed bathroom chair. She patted the indigo velour seat and invited me wordlessly to join her. She winced as the breath she tried to catch passed over raw sores in her mouth..

"Hey, Siri," I said to my phone, feeling so helpless in the face of her suffering, "play Rich Mullins." Mom closed her eyes, a half-smile of agreement flitting across her face.

After years of protecting us from the fullness of what she was enduring, she could see there was no hiding it from me now. Sitting in that chair together, Mullins's music putting into words what we could not, she let me in.

I looked on as she lifted drooping hands[16] to the words of "Hold Me Jesus" and "Creed,"[17] mouthing and emoting with these anthems of faith even as her voice faltered. Surrender certainly did not come naturally to my mom, but I watched as it began to wash over her anyway.

Afternoon light poured through the window by the time we started the shower, casting a golden hue on the memory even as it was being made. It is too tender a thing to describe fully, this chance to care for her still-embodied soul, this ability to provide a common comfort—a mere washing—in a desert of days.

The teak-wood stool she had bought for other purposes would now support her weak body beneath the waterfall faucet. Warmth and relief would flow, mercy in liquid form. And I would feel the care of the One who formed her coursing through my feeble hands.

---

16. "Consider him who endured from sinners such hostility against himself, so that you may not grow weary or fainthearted. . . . Therefore lift your drooping hands and strengthen your weak knees" (Heb. 12:3, 12).

17. Rich Mullins, "Hold Me Jesus," track 4 on *A Liturgy, A Legacy & A Ragamuffin Band,* Reunion Records, 1993. Rich Mullins "Creed," track 5 on *A Liturgy, A Legacy & A Ragamuffin Band,* Reunion Records, 1993.

These forms of caregiving are so vulnerable and raw. It's not hard to see why some would rather have a paid worker, not a family member, do their bathing. The disciples, after all, weren't comfortable with the idea of even their feet being washed by the One they had come to know as Lord. But they saw and we see in Christ's example something unexpected: humbly serving is a gift, and so is being humbly served.

"What I am doing you do not understand now," Jesus said as He knelt to wash Peter's feet, "but afterward you will understand. . . . For I have given you an example, that you also should do just as I have done to you" (John 13:7, 15).

It cost Jesus something to wash His disciples' feet, to stoop low and near enough to smell the stench and touch the filth. There's a reason it was considered servants' work. When we are called to serve through the intimate and sometimes relentless work of caregiving, it will cost us something too.

For many, the call to care will cost months and years, entire careers, and financial stability. For others, it will mean stooping to do a work that's long been dreaded for a person who might not be easy to love, let alone serve. But—before we picture ourselves as the faithful servant bending to do it anyway—we must first recall that we are the ones who need and have received great care.

Christ didn't just wash feet He knew would only be dirtied again. His temporary cleaning pointed to an eternal one: for those same disciples and for us, Christ poured out blood and water to

---

18. "Our sins are washed away and we are made clean because Christ gave His own body as a gift to God. He did this once for all time" (Heb. 10:10 NLV).

wash away sins "once for all time."[18] And so it goes with His comfort. The temporal points to the eternal.

"This is my comfort in my affliction," the psalmist writes in Psalm 119:50, "that your promise gives me life." By meditating on God's Word, the psalmist finds present comfort in the reality of the eternal comfort to come.

But we were never intended to be the sole endpoint of God's comfort. Paul goes so far as to say that the Father of mercies and God of all comfort "comforts us in all our affliction, *so that* we may be able to comfort those who are in any affliction, with the comfort" we've received from God (2 Cor. 1:4).

To suffer with Christ is to live in the ever-flowing current of His comfort. To suffer with others is to become a tributary, a deepening channel of the comfort we have received time and again. May we have grace to draw near to those desperate for comfort, and may we be surprised to find it, again and again, coursing unto others through us.[19]

---

19. "Now may our Lord Jesus Christ himself, and God our Father, who loved us and gave us eternal comfort and good hope through grace, comfort your hearts and establish them in every good work and word" (2 Thess. 2:16–17).

NINE

The Enemy That Remains

"You will have to walk through the water."
But "the King will help you."[1]

—*LITTLE PILGRIM'S PROGRESS*

In the days between us realizing Mom was dying and her accepting it, I thought often of a family story we called, "That time Mom tried to take away Grandma's car keys."

An accomplished professional artist, my Grandma Ruth[2] saw beauty everywhere—in the curve of the cat's tail and the shape of the scissors left next to a vase of cut flowers. She could convey it too in virtually any medium—even the sidewalk chalk we used to make crocodiles, narrowly escaped by leaping across patio chairs. Her heightened view of the world made it harder to accept, in her early 80s, that macular degeneration was stealing her ability to see it.

---

1. Helen L. Taylor, *Little Pilgrim's Progress* (Chicago: Moody Publishers, 2021), 163.
2. Ruth Preston Finnell's painting *Iris Bouquet* is featured on the cover of this book.

Grandma had recently lost all central vision in one eye and almost all of it in the other—and she'd had a couple of run-ins with the curb to show for it. Soon after the car was repaired a second time, my mom pulled into the driveway just as Grandma was walking to her car to run an errand, keys in hand. "Oh no, you don't," I picture my mom saying as she gets out of her car.[3]

As the story goes, Mom told Grandma in no uncertain terms that her driving days had come to an end; she needed to hand over the keys.

"They had a serious conversation," said my grandma's companion, Steve LeDou, recalling what he saw through the windows from inside the house. My mom put it more frankly: "I had to chase her to get the keys!"

The idea of my eighty-plus-year-old grandma with two knee replacements "running" around her eggplant-colored station wagon still makes me chuckle. But it does not surprise me. I recognize the same strain of stubbornness running through every branch of my family tree. I watched my mom battle with her mom for years over these themes of independence and autonomy. But I still wasn't prepared to go toe-to-toe with Mom over hers.

During her twenty years of enduring various cancer treatments, my mom handled every scrap of medical paperwork, every bill, every bit of research *herself*. She had the cellphone numbers of countless doctors, nurses, insurance officials, and

---

3. I did not witness these events firsthand, so this retelling is an amalgamation of others' memories—or at least how I remember them. My mom, the family story fact checker, is no longer here to correct me. And as Daniel Nayeri writes in the novel *Everything Sad Is Untrue* (Hoboken, NJ: Levine Querido, 2020), 16, eBook: "Memories are always partly untrue."

pharmacists stored in her phone. When there seemed to be no way forward, she would get on the phone and *make* a way. Her near-photographic memory meant she could recall the details of multiple clinical drug trials she might qualify for and, when one stopped working, tell the doctor which one she thought they should try next. (This is the same trait that made it hard to win arguments with her.)

But, by the time Mom visited us in Virginia in October of her final year, we could all feel that a shift needed to happen.

She barely had the strength to walk across the airport by the time she arrived. Her white blood cell count had been so low that we knew she really shouldn't have traveled during a still-raging pandemic. Fluid in her abdomen was building up more and more rapidly, making it difficult for her to eat or to get comfortable without having it drained every few days.

During the visit, Mom sat uncharacteristically still for long periods of time. The woman who had always raced up the stairs at the first peep of a grandchild waking from a nap now asked me to bring the baby *to* her. She slept in. I watched her pace slow, the skin of her hands and calves mottle into shades of purple, as if losing circulation. The sickness she'd outrun for so long was gaining ground on her in time-lapse. When we hugged goodnight, I was aware of each rib along her back, the way she hunched over to protect her painfully distended abdomen.

We were folding laundry the next day when I asked as nonchalantly as I could the question that had weighed on me for a few weeks.

"Mom, are you going to let us help you through this next part?"

She looked up from her phone, her brown eyes piercing behind a new pair of stylishly rounded glasses.

"What next part?" she countered.

I thought of my stepdad, her husband of nearly twenty-five years, who is also named Steve. He was already doing the duties of a nursing orderly at home when he wasn't working or driving her halfway across Kansas to get the fluid drained from her abdomen.

"Well, you're really sick lately, and it's a lot for Steve to manage on his own," I said. "Could we get a home health aide or something? Just to let Steve catch his breath?"

Home health aides had been a godsend for my grandma two years before, supplementing the constant care of loved ones, so they could rest and pace themselves for what became a long process. The aides grew so fond of my grandma over that time that they later attended her funeral, regaling us with stories of her stubborn "spunk."

"We don't need that," Mom said, matter-of-factly, as though giving me driving directions. "I'll let you know when it's time for all that, but it's not time."

I had been doing some research leading up to this conversation, reading up on hospice, listening in on webinars about when to call in reinforcements, when to have discussions about end-of-life wishes. All the signs indicated that it was, in fact, time. All the experts said that the earlier, the better. But they also said to expect hard discussions.

"Are you sure you'll let us know when it's time?" I ventured, shaking the wrinkles a little too aggressively out of a shirt I was folding. "I don't even know anything about the medicines you're on, let alone where we're at in this process. You said last week you might be okay with me talking to your doctor, so I can better understand."

"I don't think that's a good idea anymore," she said, her tone more clipped. "I don't want you having information about me that I don't have. And I don't want to have an expiration date put on my head."

"Mom..." I said, ready to correct her description of what I was asking for, ready to tell her of the beauty and value of hospice, of specialists, *of help*. Instead, I took a deep breath.

"So that's a no?" I asked rhetorically. "You're not going to let us help?"

"Well," she said, "I had to chase my own mother to get her to hand over her keys."

THE INTUITIVE FIGHT

It's only in looking back that I see my mom wasn't really fighting *me* over her self-sufficiency, just like her mom wasn't really fighting *her*. If the way I prefer to power through a head cold is any indication, I'm sure I won't take any loss of my own autonomy lightly either. But our wrestling with physical or cognitive decline is ultimately not with the loved ones enacting change. *It's with the change itself.*

"Your body deteriorates, but you're really still yourself," Steve LeDou told me over the phone, reflecting on the decline and dementia he helped my grandma face during those years. "You think, 'Why should I change? I'm still me!'"

In the middle of my journal entry about that talk with mom in October, I wrote a little aside. Using one too many exclamation points, I noted that our three-month-old was learning to grab her toes and roll across the floor. How easily we celebrate these mile markers with a baby, these steps toward independence. Even as a part of us grieves no longer being needed in a certain way, we automatically applaud the progress.

At the end of life, it's all reversed. We grieve the undoing of a lifetime's progression, the attrition of autonomy. The milestones are combatted, not celebrated. We see the signposts of decline, and we know this road leads us to the edge of a cliff. There is no off-ramp, no emergency brake, no driver we can blame. Imagine the sheer sense of helplessness, of desperation, and it's not hard to see why our loved ones heading down these roads end up taking it out on the nearest bystander.

The frustration our loved ones may feel is not just over the loss of what they've had. This anger is with death itself. Instinctively, each of us fights it. As human beings made in God's image, we know deep down that we were made for more.

As Ecclesiastes describes it, God "has planted eternity in the human heart."[4] Humankind was made before the fall, to live and not to die. This is why we kick and scream against it. Death is indeed an enemy, even if it's destined to be destroyed.[5]

"Death is not a benign passageway to happiness, but a horrible enemy attempting to keep us in the grave," theologian Michael S. Horton wrote. Even for those who trust in Christ at death's door,

---

4. Ecclesiastes 3:11 NLT.
5. "The last enemy to be destroyed" (1 Cor. 15:26).

"death's sting has been removed, but its bite remains. It does not have the last word for believers, but it remains the believer's antagonist until the resurrection of the body."[6]

Too often, Christians don't give death enough credit. Our sympathy cards fast-forward through the more wretched parts of dying to fixate on bucolic heavenly scenes, on our loved one's presumed peace. This is part of why I enjoy reading secular memoirs; they're not afraid to tell it like it is. They don't feel the need to *explain* God. And we Christians shouldn't either—as though we could.

We hold in our hands a Bible that did not leave out the book of Job or psalms of lament.[7] There's an entire book called Lamentations in which the prophet dares to voice the feeling that perhaps God is working against him:

> *He has driven and brought me*
>> *into darkness without any light;*
> *surely against me he turns his hand*
>> *again and again the whole day long." (Lam. 3:2–3)*

We have here permission to honestly describe the hard parts of life—is not death chief among them?—and to lament them. We have permission to speak about the darkness, about the dull roar of

---

6. Michael S. Horton, "The Last Enemy and the Final Victory," Modern Reformation, September 1, 2018, modernreformation.org/resource-library/articles/the-last-enemy-and-the-final-victory/. I originally read this quote in the 2011 collection of essays, *O Love That Will Not Let Me Go* by Nancy Guthrie.

7. There are more psalms of lament than any other type in the Bible. Old Testament scholars estimate that two-thirds of the Psalms are a type of lament, expressing grief or sorrow to God.

those four hundred years between the Old and New Testaments, when God's prophets were silent, when darkness seemed to reign.

Without that darkness—in the Bible and in our own lives—we would not know our need for the light. Acknowledge it. Sit in its silence for a while.[8] And then feel anew, as we were meant to, the sudden burst of hope when a light is finally flicked on.

"The people dwelling in darkness have seen a great light," Matthew writes, applying a prophecy from Isaiah 9:2 to the arrival of Jesus Christ, "and for those dwelling in the region and shadow of death, on them a light has dawned."[9]

I am grateful others were honest with me about the hard parts of death, especially during my mom's last week of life. On the morning of the day Mom would die, I shared answers to prayers from that week with my pastor, Doug Sachtleben, and asked for advice about how to comfort Mom during what I sensed was an ever-nearing end of the process.

He told me that it's not necessarily *dying* that tends to make even believers seem anxious near the end. It's the *leaving*. Then, as an aside, he added: "A last word of caution. It's good to be prepared, but death is an enemy. Don't be surprised if it still comes as a shock that can almost take your breath away in the moment."

That phrase, "death is an enemy," guided me through portions of that day that would have otherwise been disorienting. Just like the hospice nurses had given us medications specific to each of these symptoms, Doug had given me a spiritual prescription for

8. Seasons of Lent and Advent on the church calendar are annual opportunities for this type of reflection.
9. Matthew 4:16.

the signs I might see, for the ugly underbelly of death and the shadow it casts on us all.

Similarly, I've been tempted to take issue with the idea, in John 16:21, that a woman "no longer remembers the anguish" of childbirth "for the joy that a human being has been born into the world." Sure, over time, the joy of knowing and loving the child eclipses the memory of the pain. But not entirely. My son, Charlie, came into this world so suddenly, so aggressively, you might say, that I was still reeling in pain when they handed him over to me. An hour later, as they wheeled me out of the delivery room with him in my arms, I was still repeating to myself, "That was awful. I don't know if I could do that again."

There are parts of the dying process, for those who labor alongside, that are so deeply hard, so physically and emotionally taxing, they leave you reeling. You wonder how you will get through it— and then marvel that you did. Walking with others through death is a marathon you were never interested in running. Yet, once you've set out, it can be helpful to know where the mile markers are, to know that there will be a downhill section right after the steepest hill.

It may very well seem to get darkest right before the dawn.[10]

NEARING THE END

It's hard to know what to include and what to leave out about the intimate and arduous days of Mom's last week of life. Because she

---

10. Andrew Peterson's song "The Dark Before the Dawn" is a beautiful reflection on this idea.

had been on cancer treatments for so long, and the side effects of the medicine had been so severe, the timeline of her final decline was accelerated. On Monday, we were trying to get her to eat. On Tuesday, we were trying to get her some fluids. By Wednesday evening, we were bringing in hospice workers who told us food and drink were no longer necessary.

That's a lot of change in a short amount of time for a sixty-three-year-old woman known for her independence. Needless to say, there were some battles over brushing teeth and bathroom visits. Things she had done herself a few days ago were no longer doable. Suddenly, whether she wanted it or not, she was getting help from my sister and me. Suddenly, doctors and nurses were talking to us instead of her. Suddenly, we knew the names and dosages of the medicines she was receiving, and she did not.

The goal lines of each day were becoming battle lines, and they were being redrawn by the hour.

We wouldn't have known how quickly the game plan was changing—how rapidly it needed to change—were it not for the hospice workers. They were sages with breadcrumbs in their hands, guides who had walked this road with countless families and could tell us which mile marker we were nearing. The first of them, a gentle man named Sid, arrived that Wednesday night to tell us Mom was "in the active stage of dying."

This made sense of what we had been witnessing and helped us know what to do next. The goal was no longer to get her IV fluids or to get her to a chemo appointment the following week. It was last words and lullabies. It was comfort and care.

It was also a lot of work. The hospice helpers were like visiting midwives, telling us what to do before they headed home for the night. We were the doulas and the devoted husband, never leaving her side, mopping her brow and searching it for signs of what she might be feeling, might be wanting to say. The work of caring for Mom's ailing body—of lifting her upright to take breaths and coaxing in medicine—would fall to us over the next three days.

There were many peaceful, idyllic moments over those days, and I'll share more in the next chapter about the good we witnessed. But let me make space here for the hard. Because our bodies intuitively fight death, there are parts of the process that feel like a battle, even a losing one. The body our beloved relied on has suddenly become unreliable. This leaves them feeling agitation, anxiety, pain, and bouts of restlessness. This, the hospice workers told us, is all par for the course.

This is also why hospice and other palliative care specialists provide us with the common grace of medications, specific to each of these symptoms and stages.

Critical-care doctor Kathryn Butler writes of the fear with which many family members approach medications such as morphine, wondering if they might inadvertently hasten death.[11] I had these concerns too until the nurses explained that we were giving micro-doses of these medicines intended to relieve specific symptoms of the dying process. A small dose of morphine,

---

11. "In the transition to comfort care, the *underlying illness* causes death. Medicines are given to palliate symptoms, not to end life. Additionally, when a medical team approaches comfort measures properly, *care always continues* . . . its focus only shifts away from aggressive and futile technology and toward peacefulness as death nears," Butler writes in *Between Life and Death: A Gospel-Centered Guide to End-of-Life Medical Care* (Wheaton, IL: Crossway, 2019), 132.

for example, "not only treats pain but also slows breathing and relieves the sensation of breathlessness," Butler writes.[12] Other medications can help treat anxiety and terminal restlessness.[13]

The treatment that perhaps helped the most in those final days was getting Mom on oxygen that Wednesday night. Sid told us that doing so might give us more lucid moments with her, chances to acknowledge what was so quickly happening, to say what we all wanted to say. That made all the difference. Each of these workers, each of these medicines and methods, was a mercy to us in that dark string of days. They were reminders that death and darkness—imposing enemies that they are—are not, in the end, on the winning side.

WE DON'T HAVE TO "BEAT" DEATH

There is an enemy that comes to "kill and destroy," Jesus says in John 10. When we sit at the bedside of a loved one who is dying, it may seem like this thief of life is winning. It may seem like the One who said He came to give us "life . . . abundantly" has changed His mind (v. 10).

It seemed that way from the sidelines of a battle in King Saul's day too when the giant Goliath sauntered out to taunt and

---

12. Butler, *Between Life and Death*, 134.
13. "Terminal restlessness is the term for a set of symptoms that can happen at the end of a person's life . . ." including "agitation, emotional distress, and confusion." These symptoms can be caused by the emotions of the process, other medications, or by the dying process as organs fail and the brain no longer functions as it did. Stephanie Behring, "Understanding and Recognizing Terminal Restlessness," Healthline, July 22, 2022, healthline.com/health/terminal-restlessness.

threaten God's chosen people for the fortieth day in a row.[14] The Israelites and their king quivered before this towering enemy, equipped with a spear, javelin, shield, and ego as colossal as he was. They despaired of ever finding a champion who would fight on their behalf the way this behemoth was ready to battle on behalf of their enemy.

So the God of great reversals sent a shepherd boy, too meek and mild to have been called up to battle in the first place, to take on what seemed to be an undefeatable foe. When David arrives on this scene, his overwhelming emotion toward this enemy is not one of fear; it is outrage.

"Who is this uncircumcised Philistine, that he should defy the armies *of the living God*?" he demands of the sitting soldiers (1 Sam. 17:26).

As speaker Courtney Doctor taught in a message on this passage, "David is appalled at Goliath's audacity to defy God's people, the armies that belong to *the living God*."[15]

These armies, this battle, belongs in David's mind to "the God who had protected his people over and over and over again," she said. In contrast, "Saul was afraid because he saw Goliath as a man of great strength. David was *unafraid* because he knew his God had infinitely greater strength."[16]

We know that, in this story, the underdog wins. With a small stone, the unlikeliest of champions defeats the unbeatable

---

14. Find the full story in 1 Samuel 17.
15. Courtney Doctor, "Sling and Stones: Salvation Is Won by Another," The Gospel Coalition Women's Conference, June 18, 2022.
16. Ibid.

offender of God. Unarmed himself, David then took Goliath's own sword and used it to cut off the giant's head.

We like to use this David and Goliath story as inspiration to face our own giants, but that's not the main point. As Doctor points out, in this story, we are not David. When it comes to the insurmountable problem of sin and its wages of death, we are the Israelites cowering in the corner, in desperate need of a champion to fight for us.

But thanks be to God![17] For, when our deadly enemy bellowed in battle, "Give me a man!" our God sent One greater than David. This Son from Bethlehem would indeed crush the head of the enemy just as Genesis 3:15 predicted.[18] Like David, He would "disarm"[19] the enemy of his greatest weapon—death—and use it *against him* to win.

As Hebrews tells us, "The Son also became flesh and blood. For only as a human being could he die, and only by dying could he break the power of the devil, *who had the power of death*" (Heb. 2:14b NLT).

What does David's victory and Christ's greater one mean for us when we are facing our own deadly battle? What does it mean for our sick or dying loved ones?

It means that the enemy of death is indeed formidable. It

17. Paul ends a section on his struggle with sin with this question and answer: "Wretched man that I am! Who will deliver me from this body of death? Thanks be to God through Jesus Christ our Lord!" (Rom. 7: 24-25a).

18. Scholars call Genesis 3:15 the "proto-evangelium," or first gospel, because it proclaims that God's people, through one seed, will triumph over the serpent.

19. "In this way, he disarmed the spiritual rulers and authorities. He shamed them publicly by his victory over them on the cross" (Col. 2:15 NLT).

means we might cower before it, like the soldiers on the sidelines. But once we see that our representative fighter has won—once we remember that He rose to crush the head of the insuperable foe—we are called to come off the sidelines.

As soon as David defeats Goliath, "the men of Israel and Judah rose with a shout and pursued the Philistines" (1 Sam. 17:52). "They still had to fight the Philistines," Doctor said, "but they were fighting as victors."[20]

In the battle with our great enemy of death, we too are called to run in the wake of Christ's victory. We do not passively receive freedom from the fear of death. But we can find, as we turn to face it, that the battle in which our bodies are engaged has already been decided.[21]

As the New Living Translation puts 1 Corinthians 15:54, "When our dying bodies have been transformed into bodies that will never die,"—*then, and only then*—"this Scripture will be fulfilled: 'Death is swallowed up in victory.'"

---

20. Doctor, "Sling and Stones."

21. The song "You've Already Won" by Shane and Shane proclaims this principle. It was sung for the first time at the same TGCW 2022 conference where Doctor gave this sermon.

TEN

Glory Hidden Within

Those who look to him are radiant,
and their faces shall never be ashamed.

—PSALM 34:5

It's early on Thanksgiving morning, 2020, when I send a note to my church family back in Virginia. I say that we are in Kansas with my mom for what seems to be her final days.

"My heart aches to see her run toward her Savior now," I type into the chat channel where we share prayer requests. "Please pray that the Spirit in her would come alive as her body fades, and that we would have some more good moments together."

Later, between the oxygen she received overnight—and the prayers—Mom perks up. I take a photo of her gripping her two oldest grandchildren, curled against her sides, as knowing tears trickle down her face. The fog and fight of the previous day is lifting, and I can see in her clear eyes that she now knows what's happening.

Our family friends Wayne and Jan Becker, who helped care for Mom before my sister and I got to town, show up midmorning. They can hardly believe the change that has taken place in her over a few days. Her fierce hug says what her faltering voice can barely manage to convey: *This is probably goodbye.*

When Wayne prays over Mom, I feel like he's been reading the pages of my journal. "Jesus, let her run toward you," he says. "Make her ready to hear what you are ready to tell her: 'Well done, good and faithful one.'"

I watch Mom's posture change under his words. I see submission to this new reality washing over her. Though she never says, "I'm dying," to my sister, me, or her husband, we can see that she knows.

A little while later, Mom makes it known that she wants to spend the day in the living room, not the bedroom. So, with no small effort, we wheel her seated on a walker to a recliner that would be near the center of kitchen chaos—if this were a normal Thanksgiving Day.

Friends from their church drop off a ham and side dishes, but no one sits down to eat. We graze and hover and whisper. All of us are consumed with Mom, watching her change, being near her, saying what we think might need to be said, and then waiting while she rests. The room is electric with our nervous energy; if she says a word, we jump to hear it.

At some point, as morning bleeds into afternoon, Mom's eyes

pop open and she starts telling us something that seems important. Speaking clearly, though, is getting harder as her vocal cords and brain, like the rest of her muscles, begin to fail. What comes out is a jumble of words for us to unscramble: "Tell kids . . . stories . . . the book . . ."

"Read the kids the Bible?" we guess. "Yeah, Mom, we'll do that."

No, that isn't it. "Online . . . the list . . . of stories . . ." she continues.

How many times had we played charades like this—in *this* living room? We are all on our feet now, guessing. But this isn't a game. We are desperate to take from her the information she needs to give us. In return, maybe we could give her permission to stop suffering. Maybe it will help us all let go.

We know her body is fading fast, and I have a feeling she won't fully give in to this process until she completes some mental checklist. This "list of stories," apparently, is on it.

My sister and her husband, Garrett, pull out Mom's laptop and iPad and begin looking for stories and lists.

"Amazon wish list?" Alli asks. "You want us to buy the kids the books on their lists?"

No, that isn't it. Garrett starts telling a story. Our friend Susan told us to tell them throughout the day—the funny ones, the truly memorable ones—to remind Mom of how full her life has been. This one is about him and Mom beating Steve and Alli at a Seinfeld game; surely it is one of her favorites.

"Yes!" Mom says, punching a wobbling arm into the air and finding her voice. "Garrett found the list!"

We have half a mind to tell her that, *yes*, he did. But we are also still so desperate to know what she is actually talking about. Befuddled, we promise her we'll keep looking.

That night, I am keeping vigil at her bedside. It's 3 a.m. and my thumb wanders to the inbox on her phone to see if there are any urgent messages. Flagged at the top is an email from weeks before, sent to my sister and me.

"I think this was my favorite day ever," she has written above a photo of us, ages five and two, sitting on a hammock with her at our grandparents' house. In the background, a fruit tree is blooming pink under a lazy Sunday sun, and the smile on my face looks just like my oldest daughter's.

I scroll down to find she's written this memory down in answer to a question from Storyworth.[1] The company emails her a question each week—*What was your grandmother like? Favorite book? Did you have any pets growing up?* Answering them over the course of a year or two, creates a memoir of sorts that can be printed into a book. We got her the subscription two Christmases ago, and she's been chipping away at the questions ever since. Sometimes, she forwards us her favorites.

There at the bottom of the email is a list of all the questions she's answered so far, one hundred and twenty of them. A *list of stories.*

These, I realize with a jolt, are the stories she wants us to read to the kids. *Her* stories. I look up, eyes wet, to find Mom laying

---

1. If you have a loved one whose stories you want to record while you still can, a Storyworth subscription can be a great option. Learn more at storyworth.com.

perfectly still on the bed an arm's length away, propped up on a pair of pillows to help her breathe. I reach for her. Though her eyes are closed—opening them requires too much effort now—I know she hears my voice, feels my hand on hers.

"Mom, I found the list!" I yell-whisper to her. "The Storyworth stories! You want us to read these to the kids?" She nods once, the corner of her mouth turning up, and squeezes my hand.

The moment is otherworldly to me. Mom has lost the ability to talk, yet she is communicating. The Holy Spirit feels like a chord running between us, thrumming with life, helping my mom make her wishes known, helping me carry them out.

"We'll do that, Mom. I'll get the books made," I tell her. "We'll tell the kids your stories."

FINAL WORDS

Our loved ones may not get a storybook ending. We may never figure out the thing they are so desperate to tell us. Or maybe we will, but it's not the words we've most longed to hear.

Maybe you didn't really want to be the one sitting vigil when a loved one died, but no one else was available. And you're still struggling to process what you witnessed. Maybe you ached to be present for those final breaths, to walk them through this valley of the shadow—but you just didn't make it in time.

Death is nothing if not disappointing. It says something about us, though—about the utter resiliency of humanity—that we develop *hopes* around the dying process at all. I know I was surprised by many of mine. And it was terrifying to ask the Lord for things I knew were so far beyond my control:

"Lord, please let her die well," I began praying before really knowing what I meant by it.

"Please let me be there," I asked, adding by impulse, "If it's Your will . . . *and, please, let it be Your will.*"

One thing I hoped for soon after Mom was gone was to find a stack of letters we were told she'd been writing to each of us and to her grandkids. We ransacked the house, looking in all the logical places where stationery was stored, where she may have stuffed them in a bedside drawer.

A few days later, I found under her bed a tray bearing six cards with sunflowers on them, each grouped with its respective envelope. They were all blank. It looks like Mom picked out the cards, talked to several people about what she would write in them, and then ran out of time.

There are truths that assure us in our prayers about the dying process and about the disappointments we feel when things don't go as we'd hoped: One is that Jesus doesn't just know what it's like to die. He also knows what it's like to ask for something on the way toward death—and to have it not be granted.

"My Father, if it be possible, let this cup pass from me," Jesus is recorded praying in the garden called Gethsemane. "Nevertheless, not as I will, but as you will."[2]

His wish was not His Father's command.[3] Rather, Isaiah

---

2. Matthew 26:39.

3. This prayer from God the Son to God the Father reflects Jesus' humanity before the greatest moment of testing He would ever face. It does not mean He did not intend to go to the cross or was somehow forced against His will. In the union of the Trinity, His will and the Father's are one (Heb. 10:9). And yet, in this prayer we find a Savior who was fully man, who is fully able to sympathize with our weaknesses (Heb. 4:15).

53:10 tells us, "It was the will of the LORD to crush him; [to] put him to grief."

This is the Savior to whom we can turn when our hopes around death go unrequited. He knows the disillusionments of death. He faced its fullness and rose to take away its greatest sting. But the book of Revelation reminds us that the grand reversals don't end there: the Savior who fell under death's curse didn't just come out from under it. In His exaltation, He *reigns over it.*

"I am the living one. I died, but look—I am alive forever and ever!" Jesus tells John. "And I hold the keys to death and the grave."[4]

This One who holds death's keys has already numbered each of our days. As hard as it may be, we can trust Him with the numbers of our loved ones too and with the way they end. We can bring to His feet desires for a certain kind of culmination to a life—for that one-more conversation, that squeeze of the hand and knowing look—and we can leave them there. We can trust that the One who knows our frames is sovereign over them to the very end too.

"*Precious* in the sight of the LORD," Psalm 116:15 tells us, "is the death of his saints."

In "A Sermon on Preparing to Die," theologian and reformer Martin Luther wonders what more God could do to persuade us to trust Him at this precipice of death:

> In Christ he offers you the image of life… he lays your sin, your death, and your hell on his dearest Son, vanquishes them, and renders them harmless for you… He commands his angels, all saints,

---

4. Revelation 1:18 NLT.

all creatures, to join him in watching over you, to be concerned about your soul, and to receive it. *He commands you to ask him for this and to be assured of fulfillment.* What more can or should he do?[5]

"EVERYTHING WE BELIEVE IS TRUE"

By Friday morning, Mom was no longer speaking—at least not with words. Her mouth lay slack, her eyes hooded with one straining open a crack to see who was in the room. She lay almost entirely still on the bed that day, but we knew in a dozen small ways that she was still with us. A new kind of conversation and careful observation had begun.

When visitors came into the room, Alli and I would explain with growing confidence: "Talk to her. Watch her face. She can absolutely hear you."

Body language was all Mom had left, but it was enough. We became fluent that day in eyebrow raises and furrows, in the slightest puckering of lips to form the words that should have been there, in the clenching of a fist and the twitching of a finger.

Still, it was hard to tell, at times, between a face that was moved with emotion and one grimacing in pain. She went through spells that day when it hurt for us to touch her, so we surveyed and studied her expressions for clues. Did she need more medicine? Did she want us to hoist her more upright? Were the lyrics of this hymn moving her, or did she just wish she could say something?

---

5. Adapted from "A Sermon on Preparing to Die" by Martin Luther, excerpted in the book *O Love That Will Not Let Me Go* by Nancy Guthrie (Wheaton, IL: Crossway, 2011). Italics are mine.

When my oldest daughter sang "An Irish Lullaby"[6] over her that morning—the bedtime song our Papa had sung over us and we over our children countless times—I watched Mom's face knot with love and grief. Her nostrils flared, her eyebrows clustered like clouds, and I knew tears would have followed if there had been any left. Even dear emotions were tinged now by the pain of finality.

But there was also a sense of something new dawning in that room. As her body faded, the Spirit in her, and in us, felt more alive and palpably at work. There were moments when Mom's gaze didn't seem fixed on any of us anymore but on something just out of reach.

For those who die of progressive illnesses such as cancer, "the process of leaving this world and experiencing a new one is . . . gradual," end-of-life nurses Maggie Callanan and Patricia Kelley write in the book *Final Gifts*. "The dying person remains inside the body, but at the same time becomes aware of a dimension that lies beyond."[7]

People who have survived "near-death experiences" struggle to describe these in-between states, as do those who have walked with others through death. "I really can't think of words that say enough," one friend told Callanan and Kelley. "I guess 'infinite' comes the closest."[8]

---

6. This classic Irish-American lullaby was written in 1913 by composer James Royce Shannon. It's been the bedtime song for three generations in my family.

7. Maggie Callanan and Patricia Kelley, *Final Gifts: Understanding the Special Awareness, Needs, and Communications of the Dying* (New York: Bantam Books, 1992), 16. Note: I found this book on my mom's shelf with a card in it from a friend to whom she'd lent it. It appears Mom read and recommended it to others.

8. Ibid., 18.

Looking back, I realized a transition was taking place, both in Mom and in me, even if I couldn't put it into words at the time. I had whispered over her the night before that I would be okay, that Christ's work is finished, so hers could be too. I wanted her suffering to be over, even if it meant these conversations would be our last.

Now, I felt less like a daughter saying goodbye and more like a matron of honor, walking the bride to her groom.[9] I just didn't know how long the aisle would be.

"You made it through Black Friday," I told Mom on Saturday morning. Sid, the hospice nurse, had said the night before that she could go any time now. Some mothers, he told us, wait until their children leave the room to leave this world, "as a way of protecting them."

With that in mind, we rested from our nightly vigil, trusting that, if Mom wanted to go while her daughters were out of the room, she would have the chance. But, on Saturday morning, I thanked God she was still with us. And, in the next breath, I told Him I wasn't sure how much longer I could run this particular race.

But, as with most races, there is a stretch of the course that gets harder before it gets easier. I was alone with Mom when she had her first battle with "air hunger" that morning. After not moving

---

9. As John the Baptist said in John 3:29, "The one who has the bride is the bridegroom. The friend of the bridegroom, who stands and hears him, rejoices greatly at the bridegroom's voice. Therefore this joy of mine is now complete."

or opening her eyes for more than a day, she suddenly strained to sit up, eyes wide, arms grasping for something neither of us could see. Sid had told us to expect this symptom that often accompanies difficulty breathing near the end, and that administering more medicine would help. "It's okay, Mom! I'm right here," I said, trying to calm her while calling for Alli to bring the medicine. We did this dance about once an hour for the first half of the day, the episodes getting closer and closer together—and then stopping entirely.

But, in between these episodes, the new day was giving way to longer moments of stillness and contemplation. I remember lying next to Mom, studying the features of the face that welcomed me into this world. I told her how beautiful her skin looked, and I meant it. After years of being puffed up by steroids or wrung out by chemotherapies, the skin of her face now seemed radiant to me. Her body was loosening its grip on this world, yes, but it also seemed to be *arriving* somewhere.

I was in that same spot a few hours later, tucked against her side, when I noticed a sharp change in her coloring. As I watched, the pink that added warmth to her eyelids and cheeks began to slowly drain from her face, like sand from an hourglass. I held my own breath as I waited too long for her to take the next one. Susan—who had driven twelve hours to arrive the day before—was seeing it too. Her eyes confirmed what I felt but couldn't say.

"This is part of the process," she said. She was steady. I was not.

"Alli! Alli! Alli!" I started yelling for my sister, certain she didn't want to miss whatever was happening. She was in the bathroom changing her clothes and hollering back, "What? Wait just a minute!"

I kept saying her name until she came to Mom's side, to see for herself what I couldn't describe. "Her color . . ." is all I could manage. Mom's next breath sounded gravelly and crackling— like slurping the last sips of a drink through a straw—just like they said it would.

I kissed her on the forehead and said into her ear, "I love you, I love you, I love you." I don't know who else was in the room at that point, besides my sister also at her side; my eyes were fixed on Mom. This was it.

Another rasping breath and a long, long wait for the next one. One more breath, and the last traces of color drained from her face and hands. She looked, in an instant, changed. Her soul had left behind this shell, with all its frailties. As she stepped into God's presence, just beyond our sight, her radiance reached its fullness.

I can't quite describe the assurance I had of these truths in that moment. I watched Mom's faith become sight with spiritual eyes. Even as my physical ones shed tears for our loss, my spirit knew her incredible gain. "She's gone," we said, with certainty yet disbelief. We wept. Susan took one more picture of Alli and I cradling Mom's frame, this body we had loved and studied and known and been loved by our whole lives. We sat there a long while, tiptoeing on what had just been holy ground, sharing stories and inviting our husbands and children into the room.

I felt in that moment like we walked her to the gates of glory and, in so doing, got to peek inside ourselves. The glow of that eternal peace radiated warmth back onto us. She was changed, and so were we.

When I told others the news later that day, the words that kept coming to my lips were these: "Everything we believe is true."

STEWARDING GLORY

When Moses came down from renewing the covenant between God and His people on Mount Sinai, Exodus tells us, "His face was radiant."[10] Sheltered from its fullness in the cleft of a rock, Moses saw the Lord's glory pass before him and proclaimed over him.[11] And it left him noticeably transformed.

The people who had so grievously sinned the last time Moses went up on that mountain were terrified by this glowing countenance, knowing it echoed the holiness of the covenant-keeping God they'd betrayed. So, after relaying the commands of the Lord, Moses used a veil to conceal the glorious glow of his face.

Jewish rabbis use the word "shekinah" to refer to this glory of God that dwells with and among His people. It was God's shekinah glory that appeared in a cloudy pillar by day and a fiery pillar by night, unignorable evidence of His presence on earth.[12]

Seeing this sort of shekinah glory had a similarly terrifying effect at first on Peter, James, and John when they witnessed the transfiguration of Christ.[13] Before their eyes, they saw Jesus transformed—speaking to Moses and Elijah, no less—in clothes that "became *radiant*, intensely white, as no one on earth could bleach them," and "His face shone like the sun." In response, the three disciples "fell on their faces and were terrified" until Jesus reassured them.[14]

---

10. Exodus 34:29 NIV.
11. Exodus 33:22.
12. "What Is the Shekinah Glory?," Got Questions, www.gotquestions.org/shekinah-glory.html.
13. As described in Matthew 17:1–8; Mark 9:2–8; and Luke 9:28–36.
14. Quotations from Mark 9:3 and Matthew 17:6.

This experience was transformational for each of the disciples, though they were warned not to talk about it until after the resurrection. Peter makes up for it in his letters. He had caught a glimpse of Christ's glory. He had heard God say, "This is my beloved Son, with whom I am well pleased." And he now saw being "an eyewitness of his majesty" as the foundation for a bone-deep belief in the gospel he preaches.[15] In essence, he says, *I saw it with my own eyes.*

But what does John write about this supernatural experience? What was his takeaway from having seen the Son of God transformed into a form of the shekinah glory they had grown up hearing about in the Exodus story? Because "the Word became flesh and dwelt among us," John says, "*we have seen his glory,* glory as of the only Son from the Father, full of grace and truth" (John 1:14–18).

John claims that the glory Moses pleaded to see is the very glory he saw walk before him in Jesus Christ—the shekinah-made-flesh, *God with us.* And because this Jesus is also "full of grace and truth," those who are hidden in the rock of Christ no longer have to shield themselves from it.

Rather, miraculously, those who are His become living temples where His presence dwells. They become light bearers of this radiance that leaves faces shining.

For, while the glory of the gospel is "veiled to those who are perishing," the God who said, "'Let light shine out of darkness,' has shone in our hearts to give the light of the knowledge of the glory of God in the face of Jesus Christ" (2 Cor. 4:3–6).

---

15. 2 Peter 1:16–18.

The One who came to dwell with us, whose death tore the veil that kept us away from His fullness, wondrously lets us bear the light of His glory too. Those who look to Him, in life and in death, are indeed made radiant. And their faces shall never be ashamed.[16]

---

16. "Those who look to him are radiant, and their faces shall never be ashamed" (Ps. 34:5).

ELEVEN

The After Times

But, though he cause grief,
he will have compassion according to
the abundance of his steadfast love.

—LAMENTATIONS 3:32

Why is it that we feel like we are just getting to know someone once they're gone? I wonder this sitting at Mom's desk in the childhood bedroom she turned into an office during the pandemic (or was it before that?). All around me are the trappings of her life—*a whole life*—whispering that I only knew a small portion of it.

I have only ever been her daughter and, until now, I have only ever known her as *Mom*. But the cursor is blinking at me from a blank Word document I've titled "Cheryl's Obituary." It feels an impossible task, to briefly describe an entire life so recently snuffed out. She's no longer here to narrate herself to me. She's no longer here to narrate *myself* to me. *She contained all our histories*, I think, and then blink back the tears.

But the journalist in me takes comfort that I am surrounded by primary sources—journals, letters, newspaper clippings, and boxes of photos—artifacts of the life she lived and the person she was. I find in one of those boxes a thank-you note she wrote, or perhaps was *forced* to write, to her mother in elementary school:

Dear Mommy,

Thank you for letting me hand out the napkins. I love you most of the time. But other times watch out.

Love, Cheri

I laugh out loud and send a photo of the letter to my sister, who had, after trips home earlier that month to help Mom, needed to go home to start a new job. I am here for another week after her death, to wrap up arrangements. My husband and older kids have gone home, and baby Ruby is sleeping in the next room. I don't have as much time as I'd like, and I can feel the adrenaline wearing off, the layers of loss and weariness seeping in. Our kids are young, and our lives are full, and it feels like there's not enough space to process what we've just endured. And yet, we must.

The days after death become this fog of activity, a series of life-sized decisions made in rapid succession. *Let's get rid of the medicines first. Was there a safety deposit box? Which hymn was her favorite again?* There is relief that "the hard part" is over only to find that there are *a great many hard parts.* I thought death was the final push, but it has given birth to this growing grief, this widening chasm.

If caregiving is a marathon, grieving is stepping onto a treadmill afterward. There is no break in between. There are no mile markers or finish lines, just frantic movements to keep from being swept away. I am moving, but I am not arriving anywhere.

I trust, even now, that this time under pressure will shape me, *remake* me. I believe that it's building strength and endurance I didn't know I didn't have before. But I also wish I could step off the machine for a minute or two, unzip this skin I'm in that feels the ache in every cell, and forget for a little while.

I miss her. And I miss the person I was before.

WHAT SURPRISES

When Mom's obituary ran in *The Wichita Eagle* the following Sunday, I nearly called her to tell her about it. I had just gotten back home to Virginia, where—despite spending the last week planning her funeral—it felt impossible that she was no longer a phone call away.

A week later, I wrote in my journal:

> *I thought I said everything I wanted to say to Mom those last days. But today I just want to ask her about 529 college savings plans and dripping faucets, to tell her that Ruby is eating applesauce and oatmeal, to affirm again the feeling in my gut that our relationship was good, that she forgave the parts that weren't, that she approved of me. What will I do without her affirmation in my ears?*
>
> *It's been nearly two weeks. I've never gone this long without talking to her.*

What surprised me about grief was that it could not be reasoned with. I would tell myself that it's normal to lose a parent, that I am not the only one going through something. *At least I had that extra twenty years with her, and we knew this was coming, right? Right?* And then I would try to call her. Sometimes it would take a couple rings to realize what I was doing. It felt so final, taking her number off my speed dial list, but I couldn't seem to train my thumb to stop wandering to her name.

Longing is felt more fully, more achingly, when it can't be satisfied. I had never longed for my mom, for her voice and her advice, as I did in those early days of grief. I had grown up and left and cleft—only to be returned to this primal state of infancy, crying for the one who could no longer comfort me.

What surprised me about grief was how it took up residence in my body. Like rioters camping on the steps of City Hall, it kept chanting at me from within, "You're. Not. Okay." The insurgency took my immune system and the prefrontal cortex of my brain hostage too. I got cold sores, joint pain, and bizarre rashes, one after the other, not to mention the migraines. Executive function began eluding me. The pediatrician could stump me by asking for all three of my kids' birthdays at once. Google Maps became mystifying. I couldn't even remember which side of the car the gas thingy was supposed to go into.

It was like the newborn haze, but more sinister. I would wake from a full night's sleep, exhausted. Cooking, which had long been a source of comfort, became a semi-hazardous sport. I was chopping romaine lettuce in my parents' kitchen the week of the funeral when I sliced my index finger down to the nail. Less than a week later, on Christmas Eve with my husband's family, I did the same to my middle finger with a bread knife—and wept uncontrollably. Every bleed left me longing for the one who had bandaged so many of my wounds. Every misstep felt like cruelty, like this body I needed to carry me forward was only interested in sabotage.

And then grief surprised me by masquerading as anxiety. I took two months off of work that winter to be with baby Ruby and, you know, *get this grief thing over with*. But suddenly, I could barely hold still long enough to journal. Instead, I printed out the floor plan of our house and began maniacally organizing, highlighting every drawer and corner after I decluttered it to track my progress. I was desperate for *progress*.

"We want grief to be a task we can complete," Warren writes in *Prayer in the Night*. "The oven timer of our soul dings and we're on to something else."[1]

When I relayed my frantic doings to a counselor over Zoom that winter, she suggested I try "being still" instead. I had a lot of questions. *Does being still while walking count? While driving?* I sensed what she already knew: that all the feelings would catch up to me if I stopped moving, that the real work in me would begin.

WHAT HOLDS

The prophet Elijah had been through his own string of hardships by the time he escaped to the shade of a broom tree in the wilderness in 1 Kings 19.[2] He bore the grief of his community's

---

1. Tish Harrison Warren, *Prayer in the Night: For Those Who Work or Watch or Weep* (Downers Grove, IL: InterVarsity Press, 2021), 41.
2. 1 Kings 19:1-8.

sins alongside the anguish of having had to slaughter hundreds of false prophets. And now his enemies were hunting him down. He must have felt utterly alone and bone-weary by the time he tells the Lord he's had enough. Please, "take away my life," he prays before falling asleep.

How does the Lord respond? Does He tell Elijah to get up, reminding him that this is all par for the course of life as a prophet? No. He lets Elijah sleep. He sends an angel to feed him. This angel of the Lord says nothing more than "Arise and eat," as he lays a hot cake and jar of water before him. A second time, the angel wakes Elijah only to feed him again. When Elijah is at his weakest and weariest, the Lord ministers first to his bodily needs. Then, Elijah "arose and ate and drank, and went in the strength of that food forty days and forty nights to Horeb, the mount of God."[3]

Elijah went on to experience the Lord's glory and presence in breathtaking ways on that mountain and to pass the baton of his ministry to Elisha. But, before all that, God simply fed him.

I too have tasted this ministry of the Lord. When I was most tempted to believe He didn't care that the hits kept coming, someone would show up with a casserole. When the kids and I got (a bad version of) COVID not long after Mom's funeral, friends from our local Afghan restaurant left "a meal" on our doorstep—enough comfort food for a week. Between our daughter's early birth, a minor surgery for our son, a major surgery for our other daughter, and my mom's death in the span of six months, members of our church home group brought us food *so many times*. The kids began

---

3. 1 Kings 19:8.

requesting "Miss Lauren's jambalaya" as if we lived in a restaurant.

Jesus also met bodily needs as He drew people to Himself during His earthly ministry. John 6 records crowds coming to Him to be healed from their sicknesses. When there didn't seem to be any bread to spare, Jesus miraculously feeds them anyway. But when they return for more the next day, asking this miracle worker to become a slot machine for their daily dose of manna, Jesus redirects: "'Truly, truly, I say to you, it was not Moses who gave you the bread from heaven, but my Father gives you the *true bread from heaven*. For the bread of God is he who comes down from heaven and gives life to the world.'

They said to him, 'Sir, give us this bread always.'

Jesus said to them, '*I am the bread of life*; whoever comes to me shall not hunger, and whoever believes in me shall never thirst'" (John 6:32–35).

This Savior who would suffer knew—there is a hunger in us no amount of comfort food can fill. When grief hollows us out, the hunger pangs of this longing within can grow unbearably loud. This is why we want to run, to keep moving, to distract ourselves, to fill our bellies with anything and everything else. But what if we could learn to hold still, right there in the midst of our great need? What if we found that the ache is the very thing that leads us to the only One who can satisfy it?

As my friend Caroline Cobb sings, "There is a table only the hungry find . . . when need is all you need."[4]

---

4. "There Is a Mountain," music and words by Caroline Cobb Smith, © 2017, Sing the Story Music (ASCAP) (adm at IntegratedRights.com). All rights reserved. Used by permission, www.CarolineCobb.com.

Grief has shown me like nothing else that there are circumstances I cannot bootstrap my way out of. There are emotions I cannot overcome on my own. There is a pit of pain that feels for a while like it's only getting deeper, like the bottom keeps dropping out.

But the gospel tells me that my Savior does not call down and tell me it's time to climb out. No, He came down, put on flesh, and crawled into the mire with me. And, when all other comforts and comforters flee, He remains. When we turn to Christ in the isolation of grief, we see that there are already tears on His face.[5] We don't need to explain what this pain feels like. Instead, we are reminded that He felt all of this—and more—for us.

"Not only can he alone pull us out of the hole . . . he alone desires to climb in and bear our burdens," Dane Ortlund writes in *Gentle and Lowly*.[6] "If you are in Christ, you have a Friend who, in your sorrow, will never lob down a pep talk from heaven. He cannot bear to hold himself at a distance. Nothing can hold him back. His heart is too bound up with yours."

I would not have volunteered for the grief of loss. But I see now how it lowered me to a new vantage point. From here, I can

---

5. A song that has driven this concept home for me is by Bethany Barnard, "Tears on Your Face," *All My Questions* album (Shane Barnard, 2021).

6. Dane Ortlund, *Gentle and Lowly: The Heart of Christ for Sinners and Sufferers* (Wheaton, IL: Crossway, 2020), 49-50.

better see the suffering of my Savior standing out from the dark backdrop of my circumstances.[7]

I have experienced Christ in suffering not because I chose to, but because I was desperate. There was no other way through it. I read my Bible like one being nursed back to health: I could take in only small morsels; yet one turn of phrase would sustain me for a week. *"You have seen my affliction; you have known the distress of my soul,"* I prayed with the Psalms. *"Come to me, all who labor and are heavy laden,"* I read in return, *"and I will give you rest."*[8] At the bitter end of myself and my ability to change the ache within, I ran headfirst into Christ.

At the Maundy Thursday service the spring after Mom's death, I closed my eyes in the third row and found myself imagining Christ seated across from me at a table. The tenderness in His eyes felt familiar as scenes from the previous weeks flashed across my mind: me crying in the car, in the grocery store, into the carpet of my office floor. And I realized, as if for the first time, *He knows. He knows what it feels like to be broken open.*

"This is my body," my pastor read over us, "broken for you." I wondered if this is what it means to share—to literally *fellowship in*—the sufferings of Christ.[9] I wondered if here, seated across from the One who drank the cup I could not bear, I might find the strength to drink the one I'd been given.

7. As Wolterstorff writes, "Through the prism of my tears, I have seen a suffering God." Nicholas Wolterstorff, *Lament for a Son* (Grand Rapids, MI: Eerdmans, 1987) 81.

8. Psalm 31:7b; Matthew 11:28.

9. Philippians 3:10.

WHAT REMAINS

Warren writes of an entire class of flowers—like moonflowers and evening primroses—that unfurl their beauty under the cover of darkness. Likewise, "there are things in our spiritual lives that only bloom in the dark."

"I'm afraid of the dark," she says, "but increasingly I'm more afraid of missing the kind of beauty and growth that can only be found there."[10]

Yes, I think. Perhaps this is what Paul is getting at when he writes of rejoicing in—or glorying in—our sufferings, "knowing that suffering produces endurance, and endurance produces character, and character produces hope, and hope does not put us to shame" (Rom. 5:3–5). These words were written in silver ink and framed in the guest room where we stayed at Mom's house the week she died. I remember seeing them as if for the first time the next morning. I remember praying, *Lord, please use this ache.*

Our hope is not just that the suffering will one day end, though it will. Our hope is that it will not be wasted. Our hope is that the glory to come will be so weighty that it will render the pain of right now comparatively weightless. Our hope is that our present suffering is somehow making us ready for it, working in us the very endurance we need to finish the race. This hope isn't the light and airy sort that can be snuffed out by circumstances. It runs deep, far beneath the surface of shifting waves, to anchor our souls.[11]

---

10. Warren, *Prayer in the* Night, 127.
11. "We have this hope as an anchor for the soul, firm and secure" (Heb. 6:19 NIV).

Ortlund writes in his book *Deeper* that the bitterest parts of this life, if humbly received, can become "God's gentle way of drawing us out of the misery of self and more deeply into spiritual maturity."

"Pain," he writes, "will foster growth like nothing else can—if we will let it."[12]

Grief, as with other forms of suffering, gives us the *opportunity* to grow. But we don't have to take it. It's tempting to crumble instead beneath its heavy load, to feel like sand-built houses that just can't bear the weight. It might feel easier to abandon the project all together. There was a time in my own sadness when I felt like God was asking me to walk on broken legs, to keep going when I could not. *I've grown through pain enough*, I wanted to tell Him. *Can I just take a break?*

But what if the words Moses told the snake-bitten Israelites in the wilderness still hold true? What if what saved us—"Looking to Jesus, the founder and perfecter of our faith" (Heb. 2:2)—still saves us? Immobilized by the wound of grief, what if we too need only look to Him again and live?[13] So lift your eyes away from the gaping wound, away from the substance even of your feeble faith. Find again the thorn-pierced face of a Savior who was lifted up to make you whole. The One whose Spirit breathed all creation into existence, who even now holds it all together. Can He not also breathe hope and change into the deadest corners of us?

To grieve with hope is to linger, then, in this liminal space, to live in the company of dichotomies. It is to see the bags of late-

---

12. Dane Ortlund, *Deeper: Real Change for Real Sinners* (Wheaton, IL: Crossway, 2021), 127, 125.
13. Numbers 21:4–9.

night cries growing under your eyes and to hope afresh in what is, for now, unseen. It is to feel that God is callous and distant one moment and to hide in Him, a rock of refuge, the next. It is to wonder if the dark cloud you're living under will ever lift. It is to look back and see: it was the shadow of His wings.

TWELVE

This Is Not
the End

All their life in this world
and all their adventures in Narnia
had only been the cover and the title page:
now at last they were beginning
Chapter One of the Great Story,
which no one on earth has read:
which goes on forever:
in which every chapter
is better than the one before.[1]

—C. S. LEWIS, *THE LAST BATTLE*

The air that would turn steamy by midday was mild that morning as I drove my oldest daughter to summer day camp. So, under a canopy of poplar trees lining the park entrance, I rolled our minivan sunroof all the way open, creating the breeze we craved. The

---

1. C. S. Lewis, *The Last Battle* (London: HarperTrophy, 1956), 228.

wind made wild cyclones of the hair we'd just brushed, but it was summer. All was well.

"Turn up the music!" Cora hollered through a mouthful of hair from the backseat.

The *Getty Kids Hymnal* was playing—an album of young lungs belting out old songs of faith together with fiddles and Irish bagpipes. I hoped that singing along to "All Creatures of Our God and King" would prompt us to praise before she spent the day in nature. We'd usually skip next to our favorite song on the album, "His Mercy Is More." But, that morning, I let it play through.

So, I wasn't prepared to hear "Crown Him with Many Crowns" coming through the speakers. And I wasn't at all ready for the effect this song would have on me, this first summer after watching my mom pass from this life into the next. But over the din of tiny voices praising the One seated on a heavenly throne, I began to hear my mom's. Shrill at first, as it always was in my memory, and louder than I liked it to be when standing next to her in church. But now I knew why. The subject of her praise was so worthy of the crown, so worthy of full-throated song. And she'd been rehearsing all along.

I might have shaken off this daydream—this hearing in my mind of a voice that was no longer here. But it plucked at a chord of certainty running just beneath my everyday reality. It reverberated through me, rattling tears from my eyes and reminding me: there is a hope that's as real as it is unseen.[2] Just as gravity

---

2. "Now hope that is seen is not hope. For who hopes for what he sees? But if we hope for what we do not see, we wait for it with patience" (Rom. 8:24b–25).

roots us to this world, the eternity that's written on our hearts pulls us toward the next.[3]

DEEPER STILL

Were it not for my husband's insistence, I never would have tried scuba diving. I don't care much for swimming—I prefer to know where my next breath is coming from when I exercise, *thank you very much*—and I don't like the idea of drowning, either. So it was with some dread that I slogged through online trainings and quivered through the exercises that left me certified a few years into our marriage.

It wasn't until *after* I plunged trembling into the depths of that ocean outside Cozumel that I understood: there were things under the raucous waves I could never have imagined. Fear, yes, but also a peace and beauty and mystery—there was no comparison on dry land. Reefs begged to be explored. Multi-colored lobsters lurched in the shadows. Squid fluttered before my eyes like nighttime butterflies, then shot away like spaceships.

So it is with life, especially life lived in the presence of a God whose ways are not our own.[4] There are truths we know, truths we're pretty sure we believe. But the only way to be certain is to zip them wetsuit-like over our skin and jump into the deep end.

Walking with others through death can be like that, though it's not the sort of thing we volunteer for. We spend much of

---

3. Ecclesiastes 3:11.
4. The Latin phrase *coram Deo*, which means life lived before the face of God, perhaps best captures this concept.

our lives dreading proximity to this particular undertow. But I have found in witnessing death so closely—and yet somehow surviving the loss—a great repository of beauty I did not know before, at least not like this. I had read the travel brochure, but I had not plumbed the watery depths.

Among the treasures found here was an ineffable sense of God's nearness as He drew me into unknown waters that He alone knows well.[5] Hidden beneath the cloak of death were aspects of God's character and common grace that I *knew* but had to *experience*.[6]

We are, after all, flesh and blood. Sometimes we need to press our finger into the holes of Christ's crucified hands. Sometimes we need to taste and see that He is good.[7] Sometimes we need to hear the choir singing before we can remember the chorus and join the song.

In this way, what I witnessed in my mom's death brought truths I had long believed into vivid color. I had seen my mom change. I had felt the room change. *I had changed.* For a moment, the curtain that separates us from eternity fluttered open. Heaven and earth flattened into one plane. The already and the not-yet shook hands. And I sensed in part how one day, in full, the prayer Jesus taught His disciples to pray will be answered "on earth as it is in heaven."[8]

---

5. The Sons of Korah write in Psalm 42:7–8 of the relationship between deep waters and the presence of God, "Deep calls to deep at the roar of your waterfalls; all your breakers and your waves have gone over me. By day the LORD commands his steadfast love, and at night his song is with me, a prayer to the God of my life."

6. In French, there are two different words for knowing. *Savoir* means to know a fact, whereas *connaître* means to know a person, place, or thing *experientially*. I find that helpful. Also, does this count as using my French minor?

7. Psalm 34:8.

8. Matthew 6:10b.

This is how facing death and loss transforms us. From the messy middle places of our own lives, we're reminded of the end. And we get to live the rest of our days in light of it. The genuineness of our faith is tested by these fires that refine, preparing us—even through pain—for splendor.[9]

LOSS LIFTS OUR GAZE

I had long believed that those who trust in Christ, though they die, yet shall they live.[10] But, now I had skin in the game. Someone I loved was no longer here. Did I believe she had really made it into the arms of Christ?

Having a loved one on the other side left me thinking about it more. My mind was a tongue drifting again and again to the gaping hole left in the wake of a pulled tooth. I longed for what I had before, for what was missing. But over time, I began to long even more for the day when it would be fixed, when brokenness itself will be made new.

The life that had ended kept reminding me of the need for a life that does not end, the fullness of eternal life offered to each of us in Christ.[11] Meanwhile, what I already considered true began to *feel*—as I meditated upon it—more real, more reachable, more right now.

---

9. 1 Peter 1:3–9, especially verses 6–8. Also, Romans 8:16–17.

10. John 11:25.

11. "If the Spirit of him who raised Jesus from the dead dwells in you, he who raised Christ Jesus from the dead will also give life to your mortal bodies through his Spirit who dwells in you" (Rom. 8:11).

As Joni Eareckson Tada writes in the book *Heaven*:

> These dear ones take with them a part of your heart that no one can replace. And since the pursuit of heaven is an occupation of the heart anyway, don't be surprised if you find yourself longing for heaven after you leave the graveside. If your heart is with your loved ones, and they are home with the Lord, then heaven is home for you too.[12]

It is, of course, not surprising that we would think of heaven more often after the death of a loved one. In fact, others' notions of heaven seem to be the very thing they want to assure us of most in the wake of death. "They're in a better place," they say. And, "She's looking down on you still." But are either of these platitudes the best description of what heaven is and what our loved ones who've died in Christ may be doing there?

Wayne Grudem's *Systematic Theology* describes heaven, instead, as the place where "the greatest manifestation of God's presence" exists, causing the full flourishing of all who enter its gates. Here, in the presence of angels, other heavenly creatures and redeemed saints, "he makes his glory known."[13] And what do the saints do in response? "They [fall] on their faces before the throne and [worship] God" (Rev. 7:11).

So, yes, those who die in the arms of Christ enter into a *much* better place than the fallen world they've left behind. The apostle Paul even said explicitly that "to depart and be with Christ . . .

---

12. Joni Eareckson Tada, *Heaven . . . Your Real Home* (Grand Rapids, MI: Zondervan, 2018), 91, eBook.

13. Wayne Grudem, *Systematic Theology: An Introduction to Biblical Doctrine* (Leicester, UK: InterVarsity Press, 1994), 1159.

is far better" (Phil. 1:23). But that does not invalidate the sheer sense of loss their loved ones continue to carry. "They're in a better place," and "They're not here," can be true at the same time. (And need I remind us that not everything that's true is *helpful* to say to a grieving person?)

As for whether our loved ones are watching a livestream of our lives back here on earth? I suggest with great tenderness— toward the child in each of us who still says, 'Look at me!'—that their gaze is fixed on its most-worthy object. "Now we see but a dim reflection as in a mirror; *then we shall see face to face. Now I know in part; then I shall know fully, even as I am fully known*" (1 Cor. 13:12 BSB).[14]

When it comes to having their full attention, what could compete with the face-to-face glory of the living God? What pastime, what preoccupation, could lure any of us away from basking in it? All earthly loves in all their goodness will be revealed as mere arrows pointing us toward this, their culmination.

Instead, I imagine our loved ones' sentiments toward those they've left behind mirroring what Jesus prayed before leaving this earth and His beloved disciples: "Father, I want those you have given Me to be with Me where I am, that they may see the glory You gave Me because You loved Me before the foundation of the world" (John 17:24 BSB).

---

14. The Bible teaches that the souls of those who believe in Christ go immediately into God's presence (Luke 23:43), even as their bodies remain on earth. When Christ returns one day, their souls will be reunited with their bodies and fully redeemed to spend eternity with God in a new heavens and a new earth (1 Cor. 15). For more Scripture references, see Grudem, *Systematic Theology,* chapters 41 and 42.

Those whose souls have gone into the presence of God do not want to leave or look back.[15] That which lured Lot's wife and the Israelites to pine after what had been has no pull on them now. Instead, they fully share in Christ's desire to bring "many sons to glory" (Heb. 2:10). Rather than longing to be *back here* with you, they want you to *be there* too.

LONGING, REDIRECTED

At one point in Israel's wandering journey toward the promised land, God said their sin had become so great that He would no longer accompany them into the land. And Moses said to the Lord, "If your presence will not go with me, do not bring us up from here. For how shall it be known that I have found favor in your sight, I and your people? Is it not in your going with us?" (Ex. 33:15–16a).

Moses knew what made the milk-and-honey promised land a dwelling place worth pressing toward. Without the presence of God, they may as well stay in the wilderness.

Pastor John Piper poses to us a similar question about the promised land appointed for Christ followers: "If you could have heaven, with no sickness, and with all the friends you ever had on earth, and all the food you ever liked, and all the leisure activities you ever enjoyed, and all the natural beauties you ever saw, all the physical pleasures you ever tasted, and no human conflict or any

---

15. Though those who enter hell might. See the story of the rich man and Lazarus in Luke 16:19–31.

natural disasters, could you be satisfied with heaven, if Christ was not there?"[16]

After being with Jesus, His disciples did not want it any other way. They were bereft when Jesus said of His impending death, "Where I am going you cannot follow me now" (John 13:36).

Their questions conveyed utter confusion. "Lord, where are you going?" Peter asked. "Lord, we do not know where you are going. How can we know the way?" Thomas pleaded.[17]

Their hearts were troubled and filled with sorrow, as all of ours are when someone we love is stripped from our lives. *How could He leave?* they wondered. *How could it possibly be to our advantage that this One who has the words of life should leave us in the hands of some unknown "Helper"?*[18]

Christ did not explain where He was going, or how or when; how could they have understood then? But He did not scold them for their childlike questions either. Rather, the great assurance He gave to them was that they would be in His presence again. He would leave them only for "a little while."[19]

The assurance He gave to them, He gives to those who believe today: the story of God's presence with us does not end with death. In fact, it begins.

"In my Father's house are many rooms. If it were not so, would I have told you that I go to prepare a place for you? And if I go

---

16. John Piper, *God Is the Gospel: Meditations on God's Love as the Gift of Himself* (Wheaton, IL: Crossway, 2005), 15, https://document.desiringgod.org/god-is-the-gospel-en.pdf?ts=1446647389.

17. John 13:6; 14:5.

18. John 14:16.

19. The phrase "a little while" is repeated throughout John 13 and 14.

and prepare a place for you, I will come again and will take you to myself, *that where I am you may be also*" (John 14:2–3). The One who was born in a manger because there was "no room" in the inn has made room in an eternal home for us.[20]

The diagnoses and deaths of loved ones can leave us desperately homesick, feeling homeless even. Perhaps you, like me, have had to empty the drawers of a place or a person that once felt like the very word *home*. But, even in the absence of the good that was, we can take heart. These longings for the loves we've known, for the places they inhabited, will not go unrequited forever. Rather, they will be swallowed up—like death itself—in the presence of God.

PROOF OF PRESENCE

There's an image that's developed in my head, like an old-school roll of film, as I've written the words that fill this book. It is of someone sitting in a steep-sided, muddy pit, the kind that the dog Shadow could not seem to get out of in the movie *Homeward Bound*.[21] I am in it. You are in it. The grief that has brought us here is coming or has already come. It is deep, and it is dark.

But when my mind's eye zooms out on that image and my vision adjusts, I see something else. I see that the darkness I felt in that pit was not an absence of light. It was a shadow.

Shadows leave at times imperceptible evidence that they are

---

20. "And she gave birth to her firstborn, a Son. She wrapped Him in swaddling cloths and laid Him in a manger, because there was no room for them in the inn" (Luke 2:7 BSB).

21. Duwayne Dunham, director. *Homeward Bound.* 1993, Walt Disney Pictures.

there, even when we can't quite put our finger on them. There are two things Scripture describes again and again as casting shadows. One is death.[22] The other is the presence of God.[23]

And Psalm 23:4 memorably puts the two motifs together:

Even though I walk through the valley of the shadow of death,
I will fear no evil,
for you are with me.

Do you see what makes this so profound? Where the shadow of death is present, Psalm 23 says, *God is too*. How easy it is to only see the shadow of our circumstances, to believe the lonesome lies they tell. But what if the shadow you feel stuck beneath is not just a foreboding one of loss? What if it's also proof of the presence that covers you, evidence that the Almighty is near—hovering over you, tending to you, never leaving you?

What do we do when God's presence is hardest to imagine, when it feels impossible to believe? We blow the dust off the evidence and let it surprise us again: "He came to his own" (John 1:11).[24] Jesus Christ, the light of the world, was born to begin the

---

22. "We are but of yesterday and know nothing, for our days on earth are a shadow" (Job 8:9); "Surely a man goes about as a shadow!" (Ps. 39:6); "Yet you have broken us in the place of jackals and covered us with the shadow of death" (Ps. 44:19).

23. "Hide me in the shadow of your wings" (Ps. 17:8b); "The children of mankind take refuge in the shadow of your wings" (Ps. 36:7); "He who dwells in the shelter of the Most High will abide in the shadow of the Almighty" (Ps. 91:1).

24. "Trace him, Christian," Charles Spurgeon preached. "He has left thee his manger to show thee how God came down to man . . . trace him along his weary way, as the Man of Sorrows, and acquainted with grief." Charles Spurgeon in a sermon on 2 Corinthians 8:9, September 13, 1857, https://www.spurgeon.org/resource-library/sermons/the-condescension-of-christ/#flipbook/.

patient work of overshadowing death itself. For "the people dwelling in darkness have seen a great light, and for those dwelling in the region and *shadow of death, on them a light has dawned*."[25] Those who die in Christ or long for His return, therefore, will one day see the light He casts driving out every last remnant of death's shadow.

Until then, we wait. There were hours, after all, during Christ's crucifixion, when no shadows were cast, when the sun itself stopped shining. There have been hours in our own lives when the presence of God felt uncertain, like the unsteady shadows cast by a flickering candle.

But it will not be so on the day when "night will be no more."[26] For there the light of the Lord's presence will be unignorably bright. And we who have traced its shape in this shadowland will have eyes to see it—and lungs to sing along.

> *Crown Him the Lord of life,*
> *who triumphed o'er the grave,*
> *and rose victorious in the strife*
> *for those He came to save;*
> *His glories now we sing*
> *who died and rose on high,*
> *who died eternal life to bring,*
> *and lives that death may die.*[27]

---

25. Matthew 4:16.
26. Revelation 22:5.
27. Matthew Bridges, "Crown Him with Many Crowns" (1851).

Afterword:
"For I Could Wish . . ."

Our church was wrapping up a sermon series in Romans 8—that mountaintop overview of God's goodness displayed in the gospel—just in time for Easter. After walking through a somber Good Friday and the quiet waiting of Saturday, we were eager for the script-flipping crescendo of Resurrection Sunday. *He is risen!* the pastor would say. *He is risen indeed!* we would say in return.

Perhaps I wasn't the only one, then, who was surprised to hear our pastor follow this good news proclamation with a reading of what the apostle Paul writes on the heels of Romans 8:

> I am speaking the truth in Christ—I am not lying; my conscience bears me witness in the Holy Spirit—that I have great sorrow and unceasing anguish in my heart. For I could wish that I myself were accursed and cut off from Christ for the sake of my brothers, my kinsmen according to the flesh." (Rom. 9:1–3)

Paul descends from the pinnacle of Romans 8 right into a valley of despair as he recalls his Jewish brothers who continue to reject Christ. Perhaps you know how he felt. Perhaps, after reading the pages of this book about the eternal hope offered in

Christ, you're left remembering a loved one who has died without it. And the grief you carry feels more like anguish and regret than hope for what is not yet seen.

If the hope we have in Christ is genuine and visceral, then the pain we carry for those who have died in seeming unbelief is too. There is no glossing over it, and there is no need to.

In these instances, "the sorrow we feel [for them] is not mingled with the joy of assurance that they have gone to be with the Lord forever," Wayne Grudem writes. "Yet it also must be said that we often do not have absolute certainty that a person has persisted in refusal to trust in Christ all the way to the point of death."[1]

You and I are not omniscient. We do not ultimately know what transpires between human beings and their Creator when the dust-to-dust reality of death is at the door.[2] We know that the thief who died on a cross next to Christ repented at the very end, and that Jesus said to him in return, "Today you will be with me in paradise" (Luke 23:43). While writing this book, I have heard several stories of family members who showed no signs of belief, and others who believed only near the very end, "like someone barely escaping through a wall of flames."[3]

This sort of "foxhole faith," as theologian R. C. Sproul calls it, can be drawn out of us when the danger of death is more real than ever. But the parable of the laborers in the vineyard—who

1. Wayne Grudem, *Systematic Theology: An Introduction to Biblical Doctrine* (Leicester, UK: InterVarsity Press, 1994), 815.

2. If you are struggling to forgive past hurts from a family member who has died, looking to develop understanding and empathy, I recommend the book *Lament for a Father* by Marvin Olasky (Phillipsburg, NJ: P&R Publishing Company, 2021).

3. This is how Paul puts it in 1 Corinthians 3:15 (NLT).

receive the same day's wages regardless of when they began the work—indicates that an eleventh-hour confession of Christ is just as salvific as a one-hundred-year-old one.[4]

Hoping, even against hope, for such a salvation for loved ones, though, does not mean we should *imply* that they did believe when there was no such evidence. Doing so undermines the sense of urgency we have when we appeal to those who are still alive to receive the grace of God while it is possible to do so. "Behold, now is the favorable time," 2 Corinthians 6:2 tells us. "Behold, now is the day of salvation."

But it *does* mean that—when we cannot know where they stood—we can lean into the arms of the One who does. We can trust in the character of a God who is patient toward each of the humans He has handcrafted in His image, who held back the flood of judgment while the ark of salvation was under construction.[5] This is a God who does not wish "that any should perish, but that all should reach repentance" (2 Peter 3:9). This is a Father who "did not spare his own Son but gave him up for us all" (Rom. 8:32). This is a Savior who lamented on His way to the cross that many of His own countrymen would reject the salvation His blood would buy.

---

4. This parable comes from Matthew 20:1–16. But, as R. C. Sproul wrote in an article, "Certainly it's possible for a person at the last moment of their life to repent sufficiently, believe, and be justified and enter into all of the benefits of membership of the kingdom of heaven ... nevertheless, their degree of felicity [or joy] will not be nearly as great as that of those who have been serving Christ faithfully for many, many years." Source: R. C. Sproul, "Can you repent at the moment of death and still have the same salvation as someone who's been a Christian for many years?," Ligonier Ministries, ligonier.org/learn/qas/can-you-repent-moment-death-and-still-have-same-sa.

5. 1 Peter 3:20 describes God's patience as "wait[ing] in the days of Noah, while the ark was being prepared."

"O Jerusalem, Jerusalem, the city that kills the prophets and stones those who are sent to it! How often would I have gathered your children together as a hen gathers her brood under her wings, and you were not willing!" Jesus says in Matthew 23:37.

Feel the ache in your heart for the salvation of your loved ones and know: Christ's arms ache to embrace them all the more. "For you, O Lord, are good and forgiving, abounding in steadfast love *to all who call upon you*," David writes in Psalm 86:5. The invitation is there, but it requires a response.[6]

And if you are among those dragging your feet on the way to Christ—or running in the other direction—I would echo to you the words Paul and Silas lingered to speak to a jailer who was about to end his own life: "Believe in the Lord Jesus, and you will be saved" (Acts. 16:31).

Death in us and around us reveals how easily we can be pushed out to sea, paddleless and desperate for a rescue we could not conjure on our own. It leaves us asking with Paul, "Who will rescue me from this body of death?" (Rom. 7:24 BSB). It leaves us rethinking what truly matters and reordering our own days even as we learn to wisely number them. But, whether or not our loved ones trusted in Christ—whether or not *we* yet trust in Christ— death and loss can change us, if we let them.

They are cocoons, ready-made for our renovation, reminding us to ask in their midst, *How then shall I live?*

---

6. "If you confess with your mouth that Jesus is Lord and believe in your heart that God raised him from the dead, you will be saved" (Rom. 10:9).

Acknowledgments

It takes a lot of solitary (and preferably quiet?) hours at a keyboard to write a book. That doesn't mean it's a solitary undertaking. No, every word here was written with the help of others.

Practically, I could not have done this work without our dear neighbor Laurinda, the staff and friends at Logos Classical Academy, Diana, and my travel-ready in-laws, Bruce and Nita, all of whom have helped care for and teach our three children. Cora, Charlie, and Ruby, I hope you feel the same surge of delight doing the work God has for you that I have felt while writing this book. May you learn even now to trace the threads of God's presence running across your lives.

My husband, Cole, not only pushed me to give this project the time and attention it deserved, he made literal space for it. He paused his master's program and picked up slack on the home front. He pushed me out the door for a couple of writing retreats and shooed me into my office on several occasions while he wrapped up bedtime with the kids. He gave me (free!) late-night counseling sessions when I know all he wanted to do was sleep. And, unlike me, he did not whine about any of it. Cole, co-laboring with you in this life has been a source of deep joy and satisfaction. I love you.

My sister, Alli, gave me the permission I needed to write the parts of this story that belong to us both. I was already grateful I didn't have to endure childhood alone, that God gave me constant companionship in the form of a sister. But I'm even more grateful that I didn't have to lose Mom alone. I love you, sis.

To the rest of my family, near and far, thank you for your enduring support and encouragement.

To the members of Grace Bible Church in Lorton, you have walked with us through the hardest parts of living and then writing this story. When we were in the thick of it, yours were the hands and feet and meals that made God's presence believable. Yours were the prayers and texts that held us together.

To my pastors, Doug and Stuart, you've shepherded our family so well. I wish we didn't all have the loss of a parent in common, but I couldn't be more grateful for your theological oversight of this story and fellowship in the writing process.

To our home group, what a dear thing it is to live the ups and downs of life alongside you all. It is not normal, but it should be. To my late-night readers, Jen and Michelle, thank you for your instant encouragement when I needed it most. To my prayer team for this book project—Debi, Donna, Florence, Janet, Janie, Kathy, and Lori. Your prayers held up my arms when I thought I couldn't type another word. You endured the nitty gritty details of wrist pain and migraines and deadlines, and you kept praying. Thank you. Susan, how can I thank you for walking through Mom's last days with us, and for walking with us since? I have treasured your spiritual direction, insight, and companionship in this season.

To the Women & Work team, thank you for always encouraging me to do the good work—every kind of it, even when it's hard. You've cheer-leaded and challenged me to steward my callings with grit and faithfulness.

Katie, I wouldn't have had the courage to do a great many things without your constant encouragement. This book now tops the list. Thank you for bearing witness to the hard parts and standing ready to celebrate with us every scrap of good. Here's to God's kindness displayed over decades of friendship, from our days editing high school newspapers together to now.

Sarah, thank you for holding my hand as I grieved my way through a bathroom project, of all things. I don't take for granted the fountain of encouragement you are to me and many others. Kari, Nancy, and Deborah, I look forward to the day when we will sit around drinking tea and reading books all afternoon, Inklings style. Until then, each of our interrupted-by-kids conversations about what we're reading and contemplating have reminded me of a God who delights to use words. Meg, Carrie, Ashley, Jordan, and MK, thank you for bearing witness (via Marco Polo) to the tears and joys of this process. What a joy it's been to carry each other's burdens far beyond college. I love you all.

I couldn't have asked for a better first-book publishing experience than the one I've had with Moody Publishers. Catherine Parks gently shepherded me and this book along, intuiting from the beginning how it could best serve readers. Amanda Cleary Eastep made editing enjoyable, Oxford commas and all. Trillia Newbell and Ingrid Beck, my agent, were among the first to believe in this idea and carry it along. I'm also deeply grateful to other writers who have been generous with their advice along the way, namely Chelsea Patterson Sobolik, Glenna Marshall, Lauren Bowerman, and Sarah Rice.

Above all, I'm thankful for the Savior at the center of this book. Living and writing this story brought me nearer still to the person of Christ, the One who has loved me "to the end" (John 13:1). By His grace I have been changed, and I'm grateful there's no going back.

IS IT POSSIBLE TO FACE THE DARKEST DAYS OF LIFE
WITH HOPE AND JOY AND PURPOSE?

Colleen Chao never imagined hearing: *"Cancer. Stage four. Terminal."* The author shares a devotional gift: thirty-one days of wisdom, hope, and encouragement. Drawing upon stories from past saints, Scripture, and habits that build joyful endurance, Colleen helps fellow sufferers put themselves *In the Hands of a Fiercely Tender God.*

Also available as an eBook and audiobook

HOW DO WE MAKE SENSE OF WHAT FEELS SENSELESS?

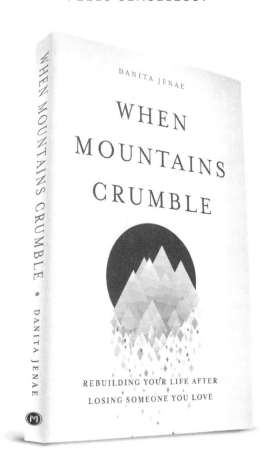

**MOODY
Publishers®**

From the Word to Life®

A healing journey through the big questions and emotions of grief. Danita Jenae, a survivor of loss herself, helps lighten your load of sorrow with gripping honesty, reassuring gentleness, and a mild case of dark humor. She braves topics like doubting God's goodness and wondering why this happened.

Also available as an eBook and audiobook

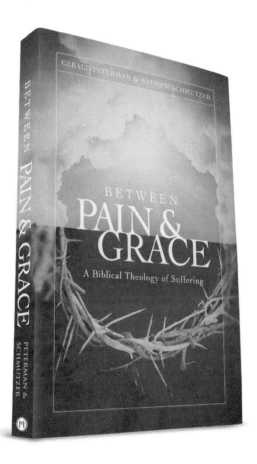